Boundary Lines

SUNY series in Contemporary Italian Philosophy

———

Silvia Benso and Brian Schroeder, editors

Boundary Lines
Philosophy and Postcolonialism

Emanuela Fornari

Translated by
Iain Halliday

Published by State University of New York Press, Albany

Linee di confine. Filosofia e postcolonialismo by Emanuela Fornari © 2011, Bollati Boringhieri editore, Torino

English translation © 2019 State University of New York

All rights reserved

No part of this book may be used or reproduced in any manner whatsoever without written permission. No part of this book may be stored in a retrieval system or transmitted in any form or by any means including electronic, electrostatic, magnetic tape, mechanical, photocopying, recording, or otherwise without the prior permission in writing of the publisher.

For information, contact State University of New York Press, Albany, NY
www.sunypress.edu

Library of Congress Cataloging-in-Publication Data

Names: Fornari, Emanuela, author.
Title: Boundary lines : philosophy and postcolonialism / Emanuela Fornari : translated by Iain Halliday.
Other titles: Linee di confine. English
Description: Albany : State University of New York, 2019. | Series: SUNY series in contemporary Italian philosophy | Includes bibliographical references and index.
Identifiers: LCCN 2018027700 | ISBN 9781438474113 (hardcover : alk. paper) | ISBN 9781438474120 (pbk. : alk. paper) | ISBN 9781438474137 (ebook)
Subjects: LCSH: Hermeneutics—History—20th century. | Postcolonialism—Philosophy. | Cultural relations.
Classification: LCC BD241 .F64713 2019 | DDC 325/.301—dc23
LC record available at https://lccn.loc.gov/2018027700

10 9 8 7 6 5 4 3 2 1

*For my father,
to his unforgettable smile*

Contents

Foreword   ix
Étienne Balibar

Introduction   1

Part One
Time, History, Writing

1. The Margins of History   11
   1.1. World-History: The End of "Outside"   11
   1.2. Temporalization and Anachrony   18
   1.3. The Ambiguous Border: Exception and Liberation   24

2. Writing, Narrations   35
   2.1. Counter-Histories   35
   2.2. Archives of Silence   40
   2.3. Narratives of the Possible   46

3. Aporias of Memory   51
   3.1. The Law of the Past: Ruins and Other Remains   51
   3.2. Historical Sublime and Narrative   57

Part Two
Maps, Subjects, Translation

4. Translation and Transition   65
   4.1. Writing Machines   65
   4.2. Global Capital and "Historical Difference"   75

5. Politics of Translation 83
  5.1. Cultural Identity and Ambivalence 83
  5.2. Language and Minorities 87
  5.3. Logic, Rhetoric, Silence 93

6. Political Subjects 103
  6.1. Geography of Dominion, Cartographies of Subalternity 103
  6.2. The Political Word 110
  6.3. Difference and Position: Alliances Located 117

Notes 127

Bibliography 135

Index of Names 151

Foreword

ÉTIENNE BALIBAR

Emanuela Fornari's book is magnificent in its clarity, precision, and depth. And the fact that the author has chosen to cite, in the course of her arguments, essays or works in which I myself have touched on some of the issues she deals with, will not prevent me in any way from singing her praises: this because, as with all her other sources, the use she makes of them is entirely original. For me it is an honor to present her book to its Italian readership (as I hope I will present it to further readers). This provides me with an occasion to measure the progress made by a new generation of philosophers whose qualities of reflection, information, and provocation are brilliantly illustrated by the author. It is thanks to them if we are all now able—and if we will be able in the future—to continue our work without repeating ourselves too much.

In the title of Emanuela Fornari's book, the two lemmas that thematically delimit the field—"philosophy" and "postcolonialism"—bear equal significance: consequently the meaning of the conjunction that binds them must be carefully pondered. This is not a simple work of history of ideas or of documentation, like the various and extremely useful existing contributions (mostly in English) that we find dutifully "inventoried" and consulted, but rather it is a conceptual *problematization* that takes the risk of generalizing and assessing the formulations of "postcolonial" authors so as to understand what they think, how they think it, and how they oblige us to think after them. Nevertheless, this synthesis—attentive to nuances, to evolutions and to oppositions, in a word attentive to the life of the research work it reports on—does not depart from an illusorily dominant point of view (something which, it must be said, would be particularly grotesque given that it deals with a current of thought that has applied a radical criticism to all the presuppositions of intellectual history, worked-out and projected by the West over the entirety of the world's cultures). On the contrary, this work distinguishes itself by virtue of real exposure to difference, and by the intense effort expended in penetrating the motivations, the logic, the implications of new discourses that have *overturned* the instruments of philosophical rationality, pitting them against their traditional use. This recognition of alterity, in the midst of the surprise and destabilization that comes with it, is not however accompanied by any servility, by any abdication of the critical spirit. The author proceeds step by step, and of the postcolonial authors *she asks for an account of their reasoning*, seeking that which creates their collective strength and on occasion divides them without any posturing, taking herself to *the limits* of what they put forward and revealing through this the coefficient of uncertainty that eats into and permeates their thought.

Emanuela Fornari's book thus illustrates a profoundly engaged conception—not only dialogic, but dialectic—of philosophy. I agree with her that this is the only fertile way for our discipline in the new conditions that "mondialisation" imposes on it: conditions that it must know how to deal with in order that it may have today a sense and a usefulness. This book will thus allow many readers to *learn* what is at stake theoretically as a result of the birth and the flourishing of postcolonialism. But it will also contribute—at least I hope it will—to the universalizing and the deepening of this paradigm. Postcolonial thought has now produced sufficiently revolutionary effects on our concepts of historicity, of "theoretical practice," of subjectivity, of universality, of collective political capacity, for us to able to face the *feedback* of its own formulations. Works that are accurate, respectful, incisive, like Emanuela Fornari's (in all truth, I know of no equivalent of her at the moment in any other language), will progressively bring to light what is at stake. It is here, after all, that one of the essential functions of philosophy resides. The diagnosis of the present that underpins its conceptual elaborations must always involve a self-critical dimension. It is for this reason that it seems important to me to observe how in this book the rigor of an impeccable historical and exegetic method proceeds in step with the boldness of the reconstructions and the absolute freedom of the interpretations and the comparisons.

Within the limits of this presentation, which ultimately seeks to be nothing more than a summary of the impressions of an early reader, I obviously have no intention of summarizing the content of the book you are about to read. To do that would lead inevitably to a simplification and distortion of the analyses within. I would like, nevertheless, to raise three questions that I asked myself in reading it and which, perhaps on reaching the end, readers of the work will want to attempt to answer in their own way, thus prolonging the movement that it has so *powerfully* initiated. The first regards the new pragmatics of the "subject" implied by the elaboration of the category of *subalternity* in the entirety of the critical work that came out of the formulations of the Subaltern Studies group, and more precisely that which might be called the "double bind" of the emancipation that this category identifies a need for, a need at once ethical and political. The second question regards the modes of the *conflicts* that model a "universalism" with no foundation other than differences, of which the "untranslatable" represents both a source of energy and an uncrossable limit at one and the same time. The third hinges on the political and institutional *geography* within which this intellectual activity operates, an activity that in a spectacular way has ended up placing the recognition of borders, of territories, of localities, at the heart of its reconstruction of historicity; thus the delicate question of knowing to what extent that which it defines as a *transition* could well be, from some points of view, nothing other than *transitory*.

A few words of explanation, then, on each of these points.

Let us begin, being as brief as possible, with the issue of the subject. There are two surprising aspects in particular that the meticulous reconstruction of the postcolonial debates and their comparison with the Western hermeneutic tradition raise clearly here—from the paradoxical delimitation of the "archives of silence" to the characterization of the identity-under-construction in a decolonized world marked by an essential ambivalence. The first is that the idea of subalternity adds a chapter that is certainly irreducibly new (but which on closer inspection was not unthinkable) to the modern construction of subjectivity as unity, which the etymology of *subjection* and *emancipation* signals indirectly.[1] The second is that only the postcolonial context was able, for necessary reasons (at once historical, anthropological, and political) to bring to light in the foreground the *plurality*, sometimes violently contradictory, of the "emancipative interests" of the groups subjected to domination and collocated in "subaltern" positions; and that—at the same time—this situation and the political or strategic "double bind" that it involves have a much more general meaning, which now tangibly marks all thought regarding liberation.

The issue of subjectivity is at the heart of modern Western philosophy: wherein it has allowed at the same time to grant freedom an ontological meaning (freedom, or the effort of liberation, is the same being as the individual or collective subject) and to make of it the key to an interpretation of the "sense of history" as progress and as an ideal of emancipation (thus the importance held by the "grand narratives" of liberation shaped by Kant, Hegel, and Marx). From this point of view, the fact that the struggles of "national liberation" of the European colonies or semi-colonies have contributed powerfully to bringing to light the *ideological* meaning (understood as mask and instrument of domination) of the humanist discourses that set up and put into function this conceptual apparatus, does not prevent—quite the contrary—the renewed attention for and the further progress of the insurrectionist movement that leads the "subject" to rise up out of subjection to an exterior authority, and to claim the right to organize the life of a community of citizens according to immanent rules of self-determination. Nonetheless, the notion of "subalternity"—and in dealing with this Emanuela Fornari skillfully shows how it, developed by the founders of Subaltern Studies from the way in which Gramsci had attempted to analyze the phenomena of "internal colonialism" of the European bourgeois world, has become object of a radical critical reworking (in particular thanks to the interventions of Dipesh Chakrabarty and Gaytri Spivak)—immediately evokes a complexity and an ambivalence of a higher degree. Indeed, on the one hand that which is "subaltern" must bring into question not only a material domination, but rather the domination of the "ideas" and of the "forms" of this domination, which can lead to an "informing" of the very rebellion it foments (here the burning question of the hegemony of the form–nation and "nationalism" within anticolonial struggles has its root, a hegemony that tends precisely to create a "postcolony" in the sense of a double camouflage of the colony that survives its official abolition and is administered by the "liberators" themselves). After all, the subaltern in the true sense is not so much a simple "subject" as a second-level subject or the subject of the subject (who reveals herself to be more often in the feminine, a woman subject), dominated and reduced to silence by the colonial order and at the same time by the "traditional" structures of power that the colonization exacerbates or instrumentalizes (with the same pretense to abolish them or with the invocation of their "barbarousness" as justification for what it presents as a work of civilization and modernization). Such a subject of the subject is often to be found in the double bind of those who have to seek their liberation contemporaneously with and against those who, within their own "community," assign them a subaltern identity.

What connotes the notion of the subaltern is thus a profound *division* of the emancipative interests at the heart of the very process of subjectivization, and perhaps also a double division: a division between the restitution of an obliterated memory whose only possibly authentic expression is, in some respects, silence (or the introduction into the story of an area of silence) to symbolize an experience to which, as such, access to expression[2] has been prohibited, and the rise of a political word that appropriates the logic and the rhetoric of the universal, affirming with this its own modernity. But also a division among the multiple, discordant voices of the "majority" and "minority" emancipations that stand against mutual oppression but never achieve (apart from in the "national" myth) the unanimity of a single "revolutionary subject," or, in other words, they can neither *meld* in the same interiority nor let themselves *divide* from the exterior. Once again, it is *historically necessary* that this internal complexity, marked by a radical finitude of the liberation that excludes all substantial messianism, has unfolded in the wake of the postcolonial experience and its painfully lived contradictions. But it is likely that this involves an irreversible lesson for *every* problematic of the subject and their relationship with history in the current world, on condition of knowing how to identify in a differentiated way the modalities of its generalized "postcoloniality."[3] The enigma of a "silence of several voices" works here, I feel, as the very allegory of what our philosophy is seeking beyond its centuries-old lexis.

These considerations lead me directly to a second question. In the first pages of her book, Emanuela Fornari has chosen to attribute to me the project of an "aporetics of the universal" that apparently takes into account the resulting suspension of evidence, for wide categories of the citizenship, of rights, of individuality (and, *a fortiori*, of progress and civilization), of the highlighting of their "geopolitically differentiated" character (Spivak). The question that I intend to deal with here is thus not so much an attempted answer as an attempt to render explicit what her analysis has taught me regarding the implications of such a project. The aspect that Emanuela Fornari has succeeded in establishing in a convincing manner is not so much, in my view, that the movement of postcolonial studies and thought is *seeking* a conception of the universal *yet to come* which is therefore relatively indeterminate, but on the contrary, that this conception, appearing at the same time as innumerable social experiences, daily practices of communication, and powerfully creative writing projects, is *already present*, functioning and active within our world. It is for this reason that the problematic of postcolonial studies, even though it may meet with tenacious ideological and institutional resistance, does not so much represent the announcement of a hypothetical culture as the description of and reflection on an omnipresent culture, *which is ours*. The world in which we now live is no longer one in which the old "bourgeois," "Eurocentric" and "humanist" universalism continues to dominate, and neither is it a world in which this last has given way to particularisms, to communitarianisms imploding on themselves, or destroyer nihilisms of every common or "generic" representation of the human (as is the reality of these tendencies) but rather it is the world of a new universalism. The master-word (*maître-mot*) of this current universalism, although still awaiting recognition (and its being acknowledged by the institutions that transmit knowledge and culture), is of course "difference," but above all—if we follow the demonstration proposed by Emanuela Fornari—generalized *translation*, with no absolute point of departure nor a definitive point of arrival (and, consequently, without a hegemonic "code"). A translation, as Dipesh Chakrabarty explains, which is always *in transition*, producer of meaning and of new languages rather than subjected to the impossible task of filling the gap between given languages.[4] Such a translation–transition, indeed, interiorizes the borders between cultural identities, dominating and dominated, through the work of language, simultaneously making of this last the very motor of the process of going beyond the abstract alternative between identities and differences. With the same basis as my point of departure, I nevertheless ask myself the question of knowing how to incorporate—dialectically if we will—into such a conception of the universal (to which, without the postcolonial criticism of our narcissistic "absolutes" we would never have had access) the recognition of the contradictions and the conflicts that it *also* involves, and which in a certain sense coincide with its very life. I think of course of the violently antithetic conceptions of "multiculturalism," which manifests today as the heir to and the overcoming of the old cosmopolitan utopias (one of these, quite rightly, is privileged in this book, because it poses, although of course it is not the only one, the most difficult and most interesting *categorial* problems: the utopia founded on the models of hybridity, of *métissage*, of the creole, of heteroglossia). But I think above all of the question of knowing how to bring into the problematic of "translations" and "transitions" the *surdetermined* communitary differences and identitary politics of religious conflicts (or those that announce themselves as such). It may be that it is precisely there that it is possible to draw, if not an absolute boundary of translatability, as the ideologies of the *clash of civilizations* would wish, then at least another modality of the untranslatable, to which the model of a universalism of differences adapts as yet imperfectly. This no matter how centered (or "decentered," as Ngũgĩ wa Thiong'o puts it, speaking allegorically of "moving the center of the world") it be on the conversion of the untranslatable as a sign of recognition (even conflictual).

To tell the truth, no matter how much "postcolonial thought," as it is here defined and reconstructed, presents itself as a *critical* culturalism hinged on the theory of dominion and of *material* power and on a hermeneutics of writing, on the story, on silence, that excludes any notion of self-referential "culture," it continues nonetheless to appear as a *culturalism*. It is for this reason, after all, that its genealogy, beginning from the process of mutation of Cultural Studies (effected in particular by Stuart Hall and those who continued his work, Paul Gilroy for example), has such a central explicative function. I do not suggest that this is an error or even only a limitation of the analysis. Nevertheless, I ask myself the question of what consequences this involves for the future of the postcolonial paradigm in the *new transition* that is developing; or, to put it in the most provocative way possible, the question of identifying that which, in a problematic of transition as a movement of self-critical and heterogeneous universalization, may only be *transitory*. Rather than returning to the classic schemes of the succession of "critical" phases and "organic" (or hegemonic) phases in history, perfectly in line with the grand Eurocentric narrative of the linear evolution of civilization (or of the "means of production"), I think it may be fruitful to discuss the question beginning with those same notions of intellectual and political geography whose inscription at the heart of cultural differences has constituted, as this book demonstrates, the strategic lever of postcolonialism.

This route could develop on several levels. One of these would consist of characterizing the *sites* of postcolonial thought, at one and the same time in terms of institutions of intellectual work (in particular universities) and in the key of national "territoriality." These sites are always essentially doubled, or divided; and this is at the root of the mobility and of the creativity that they authorize. We will notice, perhaps, that the protagonists of the discourse of which Emanuela Fornari reconstructs the questions and the propositions belong essentially to two "worlds": historians and theoreticians of Indian–American literature (and, more precisely, American–Bengali) and anthropologists and writers from the Anglo-French Antillan (or Caribbean) "diaspora" (which does not mean that she has ignored other contributions, coming in particular from Africa and Latin America). It is in these two universes, largely open to the idioms and the problematics of "critical theory" of the European twentieth century, that a deconstruction of the transcendental philosophy and of the philosophy of the history of Europe was invented. This was a deconstruction that brings back into discussion all of the presuppositions without ignoring anything of their own logic (thus demonstrating itself capable of elevating the confrontation–meeting between identity and alterity to the level of a dialectic antagonism). But these two historical, quasi-biographical universes, no matter how representative they may be, do not include the totality of the new geographies of today's intellectual work, and tomorrow they will perhaps be marginalized by the crisis of the university institutions of which they are eminently part.

An analogous question is posed at a second level, touching directly on the "heavy" geopolitics and economic tendencies of mondialisation. We will see in this book to what extent the postcolonial debate is "informed" by a reflection on imperialism and on its new modalities that emerge, as we might say, beyond the "empires." The question that recurs here periodically is to know up to what point *capitalism* and *imperialism* (or "Empire") are essentially equivalent categories, or even simply convergent: given that, under the historical profile, the corresponding processes of domination are not evidently dissociable. This question was already present in the discussions and in the criticisms triggered by Edward Said's *Orientalism* (criticisms to which Emanuela Fornari refers at the opening of part two), and it is found again in the tense debates that today arise from the problem of the interface between the continuity and the discontinuity of the "effects of subjection" (or of "subalternity") induced by "classical" colonization and by the international migrations that hurtle the poor and refugees toward the old metropolises which, no matter how armored with security barriers, are avid for "disposable" men to be used in the slums of a welfare state in the throes of decline. But the question is changing in terms of object and referent as the structures of capitalist domination delocate and relocate, passing from West to East, or even from North to South, or, if we wish, as the structural West and North cease to coincide with a cultural West and North as they graft themselves onto the new centers of "postcolonial" accumulation. Not only do these transfers of potency fail utterly in abolishing the structures representative of "hegemonic" universalism, but they tend to perpetuate them and to reduce them to their nucleus of pure utilitarianism (the one that is sometimes called the empire of "neoliberalism"). The question that is posed then with particular urgency is to know which resources postcolonial thought will be able to find, beginning with its current sites or emigrating towards other sites (in the Far East?), in order to analyze the new configurations of the power of domination and of representation: without in this relinquishing the critical relationship with the Empires and their "subjects," of whom postcolonialism has never ceased to ponder the constitutive tension, and which grant the movement its modality of writing (or of rewriting) history, its own "poetics." The fine tuning of philosophy–postcolonialism relations put forward in *Boundary Lines*, in this regard does not take place "as night falls," but rather on the threshold of a hard day's trials.

I hope Emanuela Fornari and her readers will forgive me for having introduced into the presentation of her book these unanswered questions that I ask myself. But, in truth, what does it mean to read a book, in the strong sense of the term, if not to seek an explicit rendering of the questions the book raises? I have no doubt new problems and many other questions will be raised by all those who allow themselves the pleasure and the profit of reading this work.

Introduction

The constellation of postcolonial criticism—for which this book will attempt to draw some guidelines, with the point of departure being a constant comparison to some canonic themes of European philosophy—is informed by a complex and variegated field of studies. This critical movement was established over the course of the 1980s on United States soil in the wake of the publication of Edward W. Said's celebrated *Orientalism* (1978) and has enquired and brought back into question some (suppressed) Eurocentric presuppositions at the foundation of the (Western and modern) codification of key concepts in philosophical, historiographical, literary and political theory and practice. Over the years this field of studies has significantly demonstrated the widening of its own range of enquiry (from literary texts to analysis of the constitution of cultures as much larger symbolic systems, from the load-bearing theories of social theory to an interest in historiographical practice and its methodological modules) together with the growth of figures who have donned the clothes of true and proper "founders": as well as the above-mentioned Said, intellectuals of Indian origin such as Homi Bhabha and Gayatri Spivak, Dipesh Chakrabarty and Ranajit Guha have acquired growing importance. These authors introduced into international theoretical debate themes and concepts that are undoubtedly crucial, such as the idea of a substantial "hybridism" of cultures, or the appeal to attempt a radical (and liberating) "provincializing of Europe." The "postcolonial paradigm" gradually faded out in its politically subversive drive within the cultural panorama of the United States, but it has recently met with renewed and reinvigorated interest in Europe, coming to a critically fruitful confluence with the experience (at times dramatic) of transnational migrations, the reconfiguration of the urban fabric beginning with the movements that upset (and overwhelm) the peripheries, and the more general process of the recomposition of European identity that had discussion of limits and boundaries (geographical, geopolitical, cultural) as its point of departure. In this sense it appeared legitimate for some to speak of a genuine "colonial fracture" that today runs through European societies, marking the *return of the suppressed*, which—presenting itself as a *symptom* of a past that has not yet been fully received and recognized by Europe—requires a genealogical perspective, aimed at investigating the "long run" beyond the individual national narratives (see Blanchard, Bancel and Lemaire, eds. 2005). It is from this point of view that a reconstruction of the postcolonial paradigm appears useful, and in particular a reconstruction of its most significant theoretical moments, enclosed for example within what is known as Subaltern Studies (of Indian origin). This not only with the aim of highlighting the "blinding effects" induced by a given conception (Western and Eurocentric) of reason, of humanism and of universalism, but also—on the constructive *lato sensu* level—in order to elaborate a conception of "contamination" that allows for a visualization according to new parameters of key concepts such as that of identity or subjectivity. And this while remaining constantly faithful to the critical–hermeneutic potential enclosed in the gaze of subjects who are (and understand themselves to be) always "in the wrong place" or, to borrow the words of the title of Edward Said's evocative autobiography (1999), "out of place."

In line with these premises, the pages that follow aim to configure themselves as a sort of map, or better, as a *mapping* (equipped with elements of dynamism and forms of theoretical–conceptual recursivity) organized around thematic polarities whose center of gravitation is enclosed in the hendiadys that lies in the two terms–concepts of "history" and "subjectivization." The principle of selectivity that has oriented the delimitation of the analytic "outlines" set up and explored each time corresponds, as mentioned, to the attempt to fathom, in its presuppositions and in its implications, all that has gathered together over the decades under the lemma "postcolonial": a new configuration of the "world," become materially *one* and yet today more than ever run through with cracks, turbulences, and fracture lines; a radical bringing into question of the universals that emerged at the dawn of the European Enlightenment (*in primis*, the idea of "uni-versally" oriented history). This configuration takes the form not of a mere "critique of ideology" but of a subversion—or rather, to be precise, a *sub-version*—immanent in the fabric of Western identity; a repositioning, ultimately, of the theoretical enquiry into categories such as "subject" and "identity" on the terrain of the experiential and political dynamics of subjectivization. This will not involve, however, the tracing of simple genealogies of *concepts*, but a more ambitious facing up to "figures" or "constellations," obeying the critical need to proceed by conglomerates of categories that are, at the very least, doubles (history/border, writing/memory, translation/transition, etc.). And this because of the fact that each of the categories examined, far from referring to a univocal meaning or a stable and predefined referent, underpins an entire *process*, the articulation and the conflict of which must be explicated theoretically at the same time. This condition of *conceptual dynamicity* is moreover shadowed by the very term "postcolonial" itself, which on the strictly epistemological plane, alludes to a state of transition of the systems of knowledge that does not flow into a mere need for "interdisciplinarity" but rather indicates a *transdisciplinary* program: a program that—in Said's words—knows how to evolve in a virtuous way through a constant "crossing of boundaries, a smuggling of ideas across lines" (Said 1988, x). The inaugural epistemological gesture of postcolonial criticism in fact, departing from Said's seminal work, is to bring into question *disciplines* as realities with pre-established contours, and the concomitant denouncement of the complicity between "theory" and the political–economic history of the world: beginning with the awareness that the very *boundaries* that are at the basis of academic specializations and disciplines have very often represented "an extension of the imperialism that decreed the principle of 'divide-and-rule.' " (ibid.)

And nevertheless, the term "postcolonial" indicates in the first instance a *historical threshold*, that yes finds its material wellspring in the albeit alternating events linked to the processes of decolonization, but which at the same time refers—on a plane that, quite rightly, can define itself as *global*—to a more encompassing reconfiguration of the spatial and temporal vectors that organize the experience of the present or, in a Foucauldian manner, the *actualité*. A historical threshold marked not so much by a mere process of "de-centralization" (or of "loss of the center") as by a considerably more radical and disorienting "loss of the periphery" (Sloterdijk) or, even, a condition of *mixed periphery* that destroys the historical and institutional device organized around the coordinates of "internal" and "external," or of "inclusion" and "exclusion." The time of the "post"-colonial thus appears not as a generic time of the "after" (*after* colonialism, *after* imperialism, or *after* the modern) but rather as a time of *passages*, of conceptual and material transits that redraw the territorial and symbolic geography of the world, making a place for a space that is no longer classical, no longer Euclidean: a space in which forms of dominion and of confinement, features of the colonial experience, extend throughout the entire globe, stymieing all attempts at drawing a linear cartography of the current devices of power and the correlated subjective practices of liberation and of "resistance." In this light, the "postcolonial" condition acquires a *symptomal* character in the strict sense: it remarks on something *suppressed* which, casting a shadow on the processes of globalization, renders clear the inscription of the colonial form on the very heart of the European idea of civilization. Indeed, the colonies appear as a "founding non-place" (de Certeau) of the Western theoretical-political and historiographical operation: a "non-place" that is codified as a *beginning* or *zero degree* of time and has constituted (from Hegel up to Marx himself) the condition of possibility of every historicization, configuring the entire Eurocentric historical narrative as a form of *écriture en miroir*: a history, that is, organized from its very inception on the *duty to end*. Nevertheless, it is precisely on the "surreptitious and altering power of the suppressed," on the "worrying familiarity" of a past that the present has sought to erase, that the best postcolonial criticism has gained leverage to open again a theoretical and political discourse on *modernity* in its entirety: distant from any flatly relativistic party stance and at the same time able to set out the universal categories that claim to include those social and cultural formations that are in a state of suspension, of unresolved tension: to set them out, in other words, "under erasure."

In line with this "double regime"—which assumes the semantic constellation of European modernity (with the keywords that distinguish it, such as State and civil society, citizens and individual) as a *necessary and yet incomplete* referent—this work approaches, critically, some thematic knots whose analyses allow for a prismatic breakdown of categories that constitute the fundamental vocabulary of Western theoretical identity. Beginning, in the first instance, with the concept—long deposited as sediment along the entire temporal arc of modern philosophy—of History, or better, of a well-determined *codification of historical time*, which has made of it not only the *medium* of an entelechy of universal Reason that in the West finds its own riverbed and its own point of arrival, but also the vector—this time fiercely material—of the impulse toward the annexation and the conquest of the geopolitically other. From Ranajit Guha to Dipesh Chakrabarty, to Homi Bhabha and Gayatri Chakravorty Spivak, the main postcolonial critics indeed embark on a fierce battle on the terrain delimited by the notion of *Weltgeschichte*: that is to say, by the idea of a "world-history" understood as a globally-oriented process, characterized by the two vectors of *unidirectionality* and *linearity*. The bringing into question the semantic constellation of the *Geschichte*—as a reunion, in a single lemma, of the *res gestae* and of the *historia rerum gestarum*—nevertheless does not resolve itself in the simple gesture of the overturning of the *reduction ad Unum* which, at the dawn of modernity, gave rise to the "collective singular" of History (Kosellek). Rather it aims at unhinging the epistemological presuppositions, with the goal of not only *historicizing history*, but also of casting light on the "shadow cone" that this constellation has produced—and continues to produce—when it is translated into the Eurocentric ideas of "modernization" and "development." Through a comparison with the philosophy of Hegelian history (Guha) or with the ambiguity of Marxian prose (Spivak, Chakrabarty), postcolonial studies draw a line between a purported *temporal excess* (or *deficit*)—codified under the ethno-anthropological classification of "retardment," of the "archaic," of the "anachronistic"—and a manifest *critical excess* enclosed in the need (at once theoretical and ethical) for "restoring the gaze" to the imperialist West. This is how History appears, to paraphrase Spivak, like a *catachresis*, a metaphor without a literal referent, an *empty form* in the interior of which temporal "rhythms"—sometimes dissonant—clash and articulate themselves. And nevertheless, this *dissonance*, far from leading to a linear opposition between History and histories, is at the basis of a project of theory that assumes the *enabling violation* (Spivak), the *contemporaneity of progress and catastrophe* introduced into the non-European space of the colonial enterprise, as an outline within which the parameters of *universalism* can be renegotiated. From here there is drawn up a *geography of subalternity* (this last being a term deriving from Gramsci's work) that operates as a karstic activity *within* the limits and *through* the limits of European thought. Beginning with the codes of belonging and citizenship, unsheathed from the denouncement of the constitutive ambivalence of national authority (Bhabha) and from the immediately *translocal* yearning of the movements of subjectivization of minorities otherwise subjugated and racialized (Gilroy). Then moving on to a revision of the entire architecture of the historiographical enterprise, denouncing its intimate complicity with individualism and realism, or the "royal-empiricism" (Rancière), on which European political philosophy was constructed. This up to—though not last of all—the shift of theoretical enquiry from the destinies of the Subject to the conjunctural and unforeseen dynamics of the *political subjectivization* of the social subjects: a theme that finds in postcolonial feminism its most emblematic cipher, in the form of a radical rearticulation of relationships between politics and an ontology only apparently paradoxically *historicized*.

The key stake for postcolonial criticism—and on which these pages intend to dwell—is thus, yes, a denouncement of the "geopolitically differentiated" structures of European humanism (in its declension of citizenship, of rights, of the individual). But all this departing from a hermeneutic horizon that Étienne Balibar has named, effectively, an *aporetics of the universal*: a horizon, in other words, that far from erasing the conquests of universalism that arose with European modernity, subjects them constantly to stress, recognizing at the same time their indelible *historicity* and their inescapable *indispensability*.

Part One

Time, History, Writing

I

The Margins of History

> Empire has created the time of history. Empire has located its existence not in the smooth recurrent spinning time of the cycle of the seasons but in the jagged time of rise and fall, of beginning and end, of catastrophe. Empire dooms itself to live in history and plot against history. One thought alone preoccupies the submerged mind of Empire: how not to end, how not to die, how to prolong its era.
>
> —John Maxwell Coetzee, *Waiting for the Barbarians*

> We cannot understand experiences anterior or exterior to the Occident in terms of "world" or "sense."
>
> —Jean-Luc Nancy, *The Sense of the World*

1.1. World History: The End of "Outside"

The question of the "world"—Jean-Luc Nancy has recently stated—is the axis of deconstruction that runs through the entire history of onto-theology: of that history which, directing itself to the conditions of the thinkability of the being, of the subject and the praxis, has only been able to refer to the "world" as the be-all and end-all of meaning, of value, and of truth. From Kantian antinomic logic to Marx's insistence on "worldliness" (coexistence) and the "worldly" (immanence), the "world" has increasingly assumed, *en philosophe*, the role of the *subject* of its own "world-forming," of its own "becoming world," to the point that it condenses today in the question of the *sense* of that unprecedented "creation of the world" that goes by the name of *mondialisation* (see Nancy 2007; but from a strictly philosophical point of view see Clavier 2000). Nancy's diagnosis, indeed, is extremely clear and radical: the world produces itself today above all in the sense of an "agglomeration," *glomus* rather than *globus*. A "bad infinite" of unregulated and unbridled accumulation that coincides fully with the cycle of investment, of exploitation and reinvestment: in essence a sort of deregulation of the "bad infinite" (see Nancy 2007, 33 *et seqq.*). The diagnostic line presented by the French philosopher sits comfortably within a debate that goes beyond simple diagnoses or sociological and political science maps relating to the emergence of a new and in certain respects unprecedented "global space." It instead investigates the *sense* of what might be defined as a world that has become *fact*: a world reduced to its own naked factuality (see for example Balibar 2002).[1] On the one hand, indeed, the emergence of a "globalized world," a world led to a materially unitary dimension, poses once again the problem—magisterially highlighted by the jurist Carl Schmitt, a figure fully collocated in the twentieth century, in his seminal *Der Nomos der Erde* (1950)—of the relationship between European space and world space, which is to say *planetary* space, originally inscribed in the European project that from its very beginnings saw the territorial order of Europe as a world order (see Schmitt 1950; but for a re-reading of Schmitt in the light of the debate on *mondialisation*, see in particular Marramao 2012, 107–27). On the other hand, the problem of the "unity of the world" cannot but lead to the question—this time purely philosophical—of *totality*: of the symbolic and performative power of each totalizing project manifested in an all-encompassing principle of a process of *reductio ad Unum* of differences and singularities. From this point of view, it has been argued effectively that the contemporary epoch can be represented only in the figure of a *non-totalizable totality*; of an "everything" that far from gathering in a One or in a system, simply intensifies relations (of antagonism, of exclusion) among its parts (see Jameson 1998). It is along a similar line of research that we can collocate the varied constellation of what are called "postcolonial studies."[2] And this not only because in these studies there is the declared presence of a thematization, both theoretical and historical, of the material and performative power of the "totality," which manifested in what Said denounced as the European "imperial project," part and parcel of the constitution of *modernity* itself and its apparatus of categories (see Said 1993; but on the theme of "totality" see also Young 1990). But it is also because in re-questioning the material and epistemic presuppositions behind the emergence of European modernity, postcolonial studies bring to light a condition that today sees Europe afflicted again by the violence of its very own act of self-constitution: disjointed and questioned once again by the original gesture of obliterating (and dominating) the alterity that from the beginning defined its identity. In this sense, a heterodox intellectual such as Peter Sloterdijk has recently been able to maintain that in the current climate we are witnessing an unprecedented and radical "loss of the periphery" (Sloterdijk 2013, 29), and a "de-ontologization of the contours" and a "catastrophe of local ontologies," all much more destabilizing that any discourse relating to the "loss of the center"; witnessing, in other words, what might be defined as *the end of all heterotypical projection* of the European and Western project and the consequent range of action now irrevocably global reached by its ambivalent project of "modernization." And again in this sense a philosopher such as Balibar has been able to write, "What has truly unified the planet, is not merely colonial expansion, but the revolutions, the struggles for freedom that bring back into play the 'natural difference' between the humanity of the metropolises and that of the colonies, or rather it is their dialectic that manifests in a *role reversal*, a 'particularization' of the old metropolises and a 'universalization' of the old colonies." (Balibar 2003, 162–63.) Precisely this "dialectic of reversal" highlighted by Balibar records a movement, at the same time historical and cultural, of *retroaction* of the colonies on the metropolises that marks not only the loss of coordinates oriented on the dichotomy of "inside" and "outside" (or "inclusion" and "exclusion"), but also a spatial and temporal condition of *mixed periphery* that leads to a re-categorization of the very idea of *limit*: re-categorization that affects both the diagnosis of the current process of reconfiguration of boundaries and of national and cultural frontiers, and the function, both material and epistemic, that the category of "limit" has absolved in the constitution of so-called "world-history" (*Weltgeschichte*).

From this point of view, it is a good idea to highlight how a substantial part of postcolonial criticism has worked initially at a revocation in the centuries-old matter of "geopolitical monopoly of historicity" (Gilroy 2004, 10) on the European and Western part. And to do this with a point of departure rooted in the experience of a *contraction of time* that, crystalized in imperial and colonial experience, has led radically heterogeneous temporalities to be irrevocably and violently united, beyond any linear and pacifying scheme of *reductio ad Unum* of the plurality of histories in the generality of History. As the British theoretician and leading exponent of Cultural Studies, Stuart Hall, has written:

> The way difference was lived in the colonised societies after the violent and abrupt rupture of colonisation, was and had to be decisively different from how these cultures would have developed, had they done so in isolation from one another. From that turning point in the closing decades of the fifteenth century forwards, there is, of course, no 'single, homogeneous, empty (Western) time.' But there are the condensations and ellipses which arise when all the different temporalities, while remaining 'present' and 'real' in their differential effects, are also rupturally convened *in relation to*, and must mark their 'difference' in terms of, the over-determining effects of Eurocentric temporalities, systems of representation and power. (Hall 1996, 251)

However, it is above all to the work of the Indian historian (and founder of the Subaltern Studies Collective), Ranajit Guha that we owe the more articulated attempt at formulating a *philosophical genealogy of the Western concept of history* through the adoption of the standpoint of those who have been "excluded from World-history" (Guha 2002, 15).³ "World and history: taken together, they add up to a space big enough, one would have thought, to house all of historicality. But that did not happen: several continents and their populations were still left out of history" (Guha 2002, 16). Through a strict comparison with Hegelian philosophy of history, the Indian historian aims at bringing to light those *exclusions* through which history—or rather, the *Geschichte* as a unification in a single lemma of the heterogeneity of the *Geschichten*, of the "events"—has risen to a hegemonic mode of relation between historicity and the past. More specifically, Guha highlights not only how in Hegel the "mondialisation" (or the historicization) of the Spirit corresponds to a concomitant *spiritualization of history*, but also—and in considerably more depth—how the very representation of the mondialising of the *Geist* is founded in the philosopher in the institution of an absolute *limit* between "historical peoples" and "people without history" (but on the concept of "people without history" see the classic Wolf 1982): a limit by virtue of which the latter have played the role of *primitive and absolute foundation* of conventional history and of cipher of an ontologically irreparable *delay* in comparison with the European experience (on the epistemologically crucial role played by Africa with regard to the creation of the human sciences, see for example Mudimbe 1988; but for another perspective, centered on an analysis of the "necropolitical" framework at the basis of western rationality, see Mbembe 2001). This limit is thus configured, picking up on a formula from Michel de Certeau, as that "founding non-place" which—codified as the beginning or level zero of time—has constituted the condition of possibility of every historicization, re-constellating the entire Eurocentric historical narrative as a form of *écriture en miroir*: as a history, that is, organized by the "duty to end."⁴ In other words, the conversion of spatial boundaries into *chronological boundaries* (see Mignolo 1998) is to be found at the basis of an articulated epistemic and cognitive strategy of "negation of contemporaneity" (Fabian 1983)—which is to say the deletion of the autonomous and original temporalities of the non-European "other"—which has simply collocated populations and cultures consistently in a relentless and fixed "chronological hierarchy" rather than in spatial and geographical places.

Making use of a similar diagnostic line, Guha has reinterpreted the "limit" between "history" and "non-history" as a line or a groove inscribed in historicity itself, dividing the Hegelian "prose of history" (founded on the matching of "the coordinates of intercontintental space by those of universal time—geography by history," (see Guha 2002, 12) from a dense and heterogeneous "prose of the world" that although relegated to the realm of "prehistory," constitutes, the historian maintains, the repository of temporality and narrative forms irreducible to the canons of Eurocentrically-derived philosophy of history. In particular, the Indian historian brings to light how the Hegelian codification of the *Geschichte* as "intimate common substrate" to the *res gestae* and the *historia rerum gestarum* (Hegel 1956, 60) gave rise to a model of historiography in which the "story" (or the relation with the past) is taken from society and is consigned to the *State*, understood as privileged discrimination between "history" and "non-history." With a move the implications of which have affected the entire architecture of European thought, Hegel indeed characterized the "peoples without history" as "peoples without writing," by virtue of a consequentiality deriving from his own metaphysical conversion machine, as *peoples without State*: thus instituting, with this same gesture, an inextricable link between *history*, *State*, and *writing* that relegated the non-European space into a prehistory lacking in forms of politicalness.[5] Where Hegel affirms that "the prehistoric age of a people, which is only a nation, a tribe, but does not form a state or pursue aims that are inherently stable, falls a victim to the *unhistorical power of time*" (Hegel 1975, I, 459, my italics), he at the same time reinscribes the opposition between *State* and *time*. In this way not only does the state form become the discriminating factor between "civilization" and "barbarism" (or between "history" and "prehistory"); but the very historical "writing"—conceived as documentation of the development of the national self-awareness of a people—ends up manifesting itself in a *state-centric* paradigm of historiography intended as the only norm and narrative model for the past. From here the warning, on Guha's part, regarding the implications of "statalism" for historiography: implications ever more relevant because they have been transformed into an *interiorization of the state–nation perimeterization* in the very imaginary of the colonized societies.

The interiorization of the "colonial boundaries" in the very heart of the political imagination of the postcolonial space is after all at the center of the important analysis that Partha Chatterjee (another important exponent of Subaltern Studies) has dedicated to the nationalistic postcolonial movements, coining for them the effective formula, "derivative discourse." Anticolonial nationalism ("deriving" its coordinates from a pervasive *colonization of the imaginary*) has thus been obliged to recognize that which on the other hand it contested, in this way obeying a double bind, a double injunction, according to which the colonial state's access to the "Western narrative of modernity" could only coincide with an ideological identification with that nationalism that had played the role of reason and foundation of the imperial achievement of "civilization":

> Nationalist texts were addressed both to 'the people' who were said to constitute the nation and to the colonial masters whose claim to rule nationalism questioned. To both, nationalism sought to demonstrate the falsity of the colonial claim that the backward peoples were culturally incapable of ruling themselves in the conditions of the modern world. Nationalism denied the alleged inferiority of the colonized people; it also asserted that a backward nation could 'modernize' itself while retaining its cultural identity. It thus produced a discourse in which, even as it challenged the colonial claim to political domination, it also accepted the very intellectual premises of 'modernity' on which colonial domination was based. (Chatterjee 1986, 30)

This acceptance of the epistemic premises of modernity—enclosed within the normalizing rubrics of the individual and the nation-state—was materially translated into an ideology of "development" and of "modernization" according to which entrance into the space of "civilization" would be given only through a *passage from tradition to historical time*: which is to say through entrance into "universal history" and, consequently, a *repetition* of the European evolutionary route.[6] But it is precisely on this terrain—delimited by a radical examination of the contradictions and aporias conveyed by a "Eurocentric" concept of historicity and temporal process—that one of the most corrosive aspects of postcolonial criticism now appears and which must be approached. This centers on a strong criticism of "historicism" and the correlated idea of "progress" as a *staged* process and on an equally radical denouncement of the ideology that would see non-European peoples inexorably condemned to *anachronism* or to *repetition*.

1.2. Temporalization and Anachrony

It is to the work of Dipesh Chakrabarty in particular, specifically to the volume *Provincializing Europe* (2000), that we owe one of the most articulated criticisms of Western "historicism": and with the label "historicism," we here mean the assumption of a *foundational structural unity of historical time* that allows us to classify as *anachronistic* moments and practices of the present, according to the ethno-anthropological figures of "archaism" or "backward consciousness." In the programmatic manifesto of 1992 on the "provincialization of Europe," *Postcoloniality and the Artifice of History* (which constitutes the seminal nucleus of the important subsequent volume), Chakrabarty described the "disparity of ignorance" that regulates the asymmetrical relation between Eurocentric historiography and non-Western historical narrations—a disparity by virtue of which Europe finds itself operating as a silent representative within the spectrum of historical knowledge:

> Insofar as the academic discourse of history [. . .] is concerned, "Europe" remains the sovereign, theoretical subject of all histories, including the ones we call "Indian," "Chinese," "Kenyan," and so on. There is a peculiar way in which all these other histories tend to become variations on a master narrative that could be called "the history of Europe." (Chakrabarty 2000, 27)

The exclusions and omissions on which history, as a discipline, builds its own edifice thus appear as something quite different from a mere differential recording of "events," revealing rather exquisitely *epistemological* exclusions: exclusions in relation to which the prefix *pre-* (prefix that is used throughout the various analyses orientated disciplinarily on the *pre-*modern or *pre-*capitalistic societies) is an echo of a relation not only (and not very) chronological, but rather (and much more profoundly) theoretical. Europe—a figure of the imaginary rather than a geographically codified or codifiable space—indeed appears as the only *theoretically intelligible* subject with regard to "histories" and modalities of "being human" that form the object of investigation, verification of which manifests only on the empirical plane (on the "immanent teleology" that in the history of Europe transforms, according to a necessary and necessitating logic, the world into "spirit" see, classically, Husserl 1954; but on Europe as paradoxical "universal singular" see also Derrida 1991). If philosophy has depicted the European space as an exclusive medium of the entelechy of universal Reason, this has come about not only because it has played the role of subterranean self-awareness of the social sciences, but also because—as Spivak highlighted in a fruitful analysis of the Marxian category of "Asiatic Mode of Production"—it has at the same time provided a powerful functional vehicle for the Eurocentric and normative narrativization of history. In other words: at every occurrence of "Orient" there is a dissimulation of the geopolitical alterity in the guise of the empirical that belies the disturbance deriving from questioning the unidirectionality of what becomes history:

> The Asiatic mode of production marks a venerable moment in theorizing the other. The usual way of accounting for it is to say that Marx and Engels came up with this phrase precisely in answer to the question: why did the normative logic of Capital not determine itself in the same way everywhere? Or, more "theoretically," is the history of the world uni- or multi-linear? Like Rousseau's question about the origin of languages, the question that led to the largely unsatisfactory formulation of the Asiatic Mode of Production is: why is there difference? Why is "Europe" not the only self-identical "same?" Why is there "Asia?" It is well known that "Asia" in this formulation soon lost any resemblance to any empirically recognizable space. (Spivak 1999, 72)

It is indeed a similar question regarding the *unilinearity* or the *multilinearity* of history that constitutes the crux of the theoretical and historiographical program set out by Chakrabarty under the banner of the "provincialization of Europe." Nevertheless, the previously mentioned manifesto of 1992 that was dedicated to this project concluded with an appeal for a *politics of despair* and at the same time with the recording of an *impossibility*: the impossibility of a history that in making its own repressive strategies and practices visible, looks in the direction of its own disappearance while contemporaneously indicating that which resists and escapes those strategies: whether this be the other, the difference, or the subaltern. In the book *Provincializing Europe*, Chakrabarty conversely adopts a "deconstructive" register, collocating himself in a *contradictory* relation with European social and political thought and reconfiguring postcolonial research as a critical re-crossing of the "universals" (history, politics, citizenship) that constitute the fundamentals of the social sciences, beginning with the awareness of their *simultaneous indispensability and inadequacy* for the postcolonial space (see Chakrabarty 2000, 6). *Indispensability* due not only to the logic of global uniformity that unfolds under the banner of capital, but also the acknowledgment that anticolonialist criticism itself has only been possible as a consequence (albeit partially) of the European Enlightenment. And *inadequacy* because those very universals (such as citizenship and the individual, public sphere, and civil society) that are the object of deconstruction carry within themselves the indelible mark of their place of origin, always at risk of becoming the vehicle of a new—and more subtle—form of colonization of the non-Western imaginary. From this point of view, criticism of "historicism" aims not only at *historicizing history* as a discipline, but also at revoking and questioning the very codification of historical time that is at the foundation of the act of historicizing: indeed, the *cumulative–linear paradigm of historical time*, which manifested first in the Hegelian idea of *Weltgeschichte* or "world-history" and then in the Eurocentric ideologies of "development" and "modernization," is principally "historicist."

From this point of view, it is worthwhile dwelling briefly on a consideration of the modalities according to which the establishment of the temporal order of modernity was reconstructed by the twentieth-century *Begriffsgeschichte*, and in particular by the work of a historian of the caliber of Reinhart Koselleck. And this because of the fact that in this reconstruction there is indeed a new conception (self-reflective) of time as *strength*: which is to say as an ontologically productive factor. In a now famous collection of essays, Koselleck indeed had identified in the emergence of a series of "collective singulars" and "concepts of movement" (history, revolution, progress, decadence) that had appeared at the end of the 1700s, a true and proper "temporalization" (*Verzeitlichung*) of the semantic content of the categories through which modernity acquired its characteristic orientation toward the future (see Koselleck 2004; but on this theme see also Marramao 2005). In particular, Koselleck saw in the emergence of the "collective singular" of "history" (*die Geschichte*) not only the re-union, in a single lemma, of the *res gestae* and of the *historia rerum gestarum*, of the *pragmata* and the "recounts" of historical stories, but also the emergence of a sort of "metaconcept" that brought a unity to all the single past histories and those possible in the future. In other words, through a sort of "transcendental turn," with the *Geschichte* imposing itself—and, even more so, with the Hegelian *Weltgeschichte*—history (as *logic of history*) becomes "the subject of its own self," thematizing not only events that empirically took place, but above all "the conditions of possible histories" (Koselleck 2006, 75).

It is precisely around this figure of history as a metaconcept on which a *linear, progressive, cumulative,* and *exemplary* image of historical time is arranged, that Chakrabarty's corrosive criticism of the "historicist" thought of modern Europe unfolds. The Indian historian shows how the politicization of the populations and the advent of "political modernity" beyond the Western capitalistic democracies has indeed led to a *pluralization of the history of power* that questions at its very root the "historicist" epistemological framework abridged in the formula: "first in Europe and then elsewhere" (see Chakrabatry 2000, 8 *et seqq.*). This historicist scheme takes its form (from John Stuart Mill up to Marx himself) from a "not yet" communicated by Europe to the colonized peoples: which is to say a *continual dilation of the time* of independence and of self-government linked to the achievement of a presumed capacity to "govern themselves by themselves." To this "not yet" dimension—a symbolic marker of the presumed historical interval of civilization that confined the non-European space into an imaginary "waiting-room of history"—Chakrabarty counterposes the urgency of "now" as a dimension in which the movements and the battles for autonomy unfold: beginning with the crucial twentieth-century phenomenon of the introduction into the political sphere of subjects who appeared unprepared for the doctrinal and conceptual aspects of citizenship according to the criteria of classic liberalism. But his view begins also (and above all) with the theoretical claim under which being *human* "is not only to have the *capacity* to be political; it *is* to be political" (Chakrabarty 2003, 139). The field of tension between "not yet" and "now" is thus recodified by the Indian historian as polarization between a "History 1" (which is to say a Benjamin-like time, "homogeneous and empty" of historicism) and the diversified "Histories 2" or "subaltern pasts," which, suppressed by historians and by the dominant political thought alike, represent just as many "histories of belonging" irreducible to the centuries-old and institutional codes of the politician (see

Chakrabarty 2000, 114 *et seqq.*). At stake here, on reflection, is a reconceptualization of the *present* itself, beyond any additional and cumulative concept of "totality" or "unity": a reconceptualization that insists on the constitutive *heterotemporality* of the modern subject and on the dynamic coexistence, in the same social and cultural present, of a *plurality* of historical times marked by specific forms of dominance and correspondent practices of liberation. Chatterjee writes along analogous lines:

> Empty homogeneous time is the utopian time of capital. It linearly connects past, present, and future, creating the possibility for all of those historicist imaginings of identity, nationhood, progress and so on that Anderson, along with many others, have made familiar to us. But empty homogeneous time is not located anywhere in real space—it is utopian. The real space of modern life consists of heterotopia [. . .] Time here is heterogeneous, unevenly dense. [. . .] It is possible to cite many examples from the postcolonial world that suggest the presence of a dense and heterogeneous time. In those places, one could show industrial capitalists delaying the closing of a business deal because they hadn't yet heard from their respective astrologers, or industrial workers who would not touch a new machine until it had been consecrated with appropriate religious rites, or voters who would set fire to themselves to mourn the defeat of their favorite leader, or ministers who openly boast of having secured more jobs for people from their own clan and having kept the others out. To call this the co-presence of several times—the time of the modern and the times of the pre-modern—is only to endorse the utopianism of Western modernity. Much recent ethnographic work has established that these "other" times are not mere survivors from a pre-modern past: they are new products of the encounter with modernity itself. One must, therefore, call it the heterogeneous time of modernity. (Chatterjee 2004, 6–7)

Adopting the point of view of a time that is not yet historicistically "homogeneous and empty," but is—as Chatterjee writes evocatively—"heterogeneous and full," the non-Western "marginality" appears no longer as external to or residual of the historicizing power of modernity, but as an *in-between* space that rather than being a point in a process of "stages," constitutes a *place of paradoxes* that puts the Eurocentric paradigm of modernization into checkmate. Such a reconfiguration of "marginality" as—to express it together with Homi Bhabha—an *in-between* space, as a dislocating presence with regard to the universalizing narratives of Western historicism, nevertheless inevitably recalls the function played by the concept of Nation–State in the configuration of the postcolonial world. And this to the extent to which, as argued again by Chatterjee, only a universalization of the nation–form as unique *political* community was able to lead to a radical substantialization of the cultural differences, degraded in this way to marginality and being outnumbered or, even more so, to "minorities" (see Chatterjee 1993). But in order to understand the role that the state–nation imaginary has played out in the formation of the postcolonial space—and above all the strength of the violation enclosed in the deconstruction and the de-centering of its constitutive elements—it is useful to consider the irreducibly ambivalent means by which two crucial concepts (historical and epistemological at one and the same time) have been and are still "operationalized": *boundary* and *border*.

1.3. The Ambiguous Border: Exception and Liberation

The limit—or the boundary—as symbolic form and strength, is articulated in a double modality, vertical and horizontal at the same time. If, as we have seen, a part of postcolonial criticism concentrates on the "verticalizing" function of the limit, as an instance of production and of legitimation of the Western narrative on "universal history," another part of it assumes instead as its own focus of investigation the *lato sensu* "horizontal" function of the limit: understood as operator of the state–nation configuration and compartmentalization of the globe. Given the contemporary spread of the sociological and politological debate on the state–nation and its crisis in relation to the problematics (theoretical and historical) of boundaries, it is useful to use the statute of the category of boundary that is simultaneously *epistemological and ontological* as our point of departure. As demonstrated by Étienne Balibar, the notion of frontier—or of border[7]—is indeed inevitably both concept and image or, more precisely, a *beyond* of the concept and the image that constitutes the condition of possibility of every definition, itself due to this holding an insurmountable relation with the very idea of the *thinkable*: "The idea of a simple definition of what constitutes a border is, by definition, absurd: to mark out a border is, precisely, to define a territory, to delimit it, and so to register the identity of that territory, or confer one upon it. Conversely, however, to define or identify in general is nothing other than to trace a border, to assign boundaries [. . .] what can be *demarcated*, *defined*, and *determined* maintains a constitutive relation with what can be *thought*. Putting into question the notion of the border [. . .] thus always in some sense implies a confrontation with the impossible limit of an autodetermination, a *Selbstbestimmung* of thought. It implies an effort to conceptualize the line *on which we think*, the condition of possibility or 'the hidden art' of distributions and delimitations" (Balibar 2002, 76–88). Further to this: the very act of inscribing a boundary (*horos*, *finis*, *Grenze*, *border*, *confine*) as an act of *institution* that delimits the region of the "thinkable" and of the "identifiable," is the support and the operator of a *partition* (*partage*) *of the universal* that has materially led to a short circuit between the empirical dimension and the transcendental dimension. And this to the extent in which the speculative decision on what it means to define an "interior" and an "exterior" cannot but translate itself into a complex and powerful device of inclusion and exclusion that codifies the historical parameters of belonging and of national citizenship. From this point of view, boundaries and limits are not configured as simple lines drawn on the geographical map, but they possess the constitutively ambivalent status of an interface that intervenes in the processes of territorial and symbolic appropriation and division, referring on the one hand to the larger question of the *institution* of identities (national, cultural, social) and on the other to the criteria of regulation of belonging to a state or national order on the basis of a precise codification of what is valid as "inside" (inclusion) and as "outside" (exclusion). It is precisely in a similar point of tension and intersection between territorial (or material) dimension and symbolic (or identitary) dimension that postcolonial studies sit and operate a radical revision of categories such as borders, motherland (homeland, *Heimat*) and "national culture," adopting as their perspective the "privileged" experiences of diaspora, of exile and migration (but on the centrality of the category of exile and its epistemological role see, above all, Said 2000).

The first gesture of postcolonial criticism regarding a reconsideration of the wider problem of the state–nation was made in tracing the "powerful historical idea" of the nation to its place of origin (Europe, the West) in contrast with, to borrow the words of Partha Chatterjee, the "recent amnesia on the origins of nationalism" and the consequent exoticization (or "orientalization") of the nationalist drives, and, even more so, the ethno–nationalist drives (see Chatterjee 1993, 4).[8] It is in this sense that the nation can be defined as "one of the major structures of ideological ambivalence within the cultural representations of 'modernity' " (Bhabha, ed. 1990, 4), analysis of which constitutes an essential premise for a project aiming to elaborate an "ethnography of the contemporary." The linguistic–psychoanalytic category of *ambivalence* is after all at the center of the very real deconstruction of the parameters of national spatiality and temporality carried out by Bhabha, in direct comparison not only with the disintegration of the experience of the nation as a stabilizing force and a measure of social synchrony, but also—in the theoretical ambit—with the crucial analyses of Benedict Anderson on national space as "imagined community" (Anderson 1983)—which is to say as a social and cultural space literally *imagined into existence*. Pushing Anderson's diagnosis on the statute in the strictly "metaphorical" sense of the space–nation to an extreme point, Bhabha indeed reinterprets national adhesion as an eminently *textual* and *narrative* affiliation, tormented and hollowed out in its interior by the constitutive incompleteness of the processes of cultural signification and the impossible "closure" (*cloture*) of the "textuality":

> To study the nation through its narrative address does not merely draw attention to its language and rhetoric; it also attempts to alter the conceptual object itself. If the problematic "closure" of textuality questions the "totalization" of national culture, then its positive value lies in displaying the wide dissemination through which we construct the field of meanings and symbols associated with national life. (Bhabha, ed. 1990, 3)

Bhabha is against all forms of "ethno-territorial thought" rooted in processes of normalization and territorialization of identities through the link (held to be constitutive) between birth, citizenship, ethnic affiliation, and national identity. He affirms the "impossible unity of the nation as a symbolic force" (ibid., 1). By virtue of its being first of all a "narrative strategy" (or, from Derrida's point of view, a "product of writing"), the nation is indeed constantly in tumult and put under tension by the oscillation between heterogeneous vocabularies and the emergence of "interstitial temporalities" that interrupt its linear narration and unhinge its homogeneous temporality. In Bhabha's view the "continuous and cumulative" time of the *pedagogic* (which is to say a principle of *reductio ad Unum* that manifests in the "realistic" modalities of the national narrative) is accompanied by the "repetitive and recursive" time of the *performative*. This last is based on the necessity of a constant re-signification of belonging (the nation as "daily plebiscite" that Ernest Renan spoke of) and opens up space for metonymic shifts and movements through which the "margins" can have a voice (see ibid., 291 *et seqq.*). In this way the Indian critic brings into focus not only the *double time*, or rather the "dialectic without synthesis" among the various temporalities—modern, colonial, postcolonial—that block all linear and progressive narratives of the nation, but also the *constitutive division* of the national subject: a division by virtue of which the "people" is both *object* of a nationalist "pedagogy" that leads it again and constantly to the unity of a social body, as well as *subject* of autonomous processes of signification and of counternarrative that continually evoke and cancel the totalizing boundaries of the nation. Nevertheless, from a similar "temporalization" of the state–nation configuration, there cannot but follow a concomitant re-thematization of the notions (and the function) of boundaries and borders. The borders of the nation, indeed, appear here above all as *thresholds of meaning* that are constantly crossed, cancelled and translated in the processes of cultural signification, where the effect of any "incomplete signification" is a transformation of boundaries and limits into *in-between spaces* in which and through which the significance of political and cultural authority are negotiated:

> Once the liminality of the nation-space is established, and its "difference" is turned from the boundary "outside" to its finitude "within," the threat of cultural difference is no longer a problem of "other" people. It becomes a question of the otherness of the people-as-one. (Bhabha, ed. 1990, 301.)

The boundary having become *within* thus divides the national space, showing how the "other face" of the monocentric fantasy of the "people-as-one" sits in the strategic formation of social minorities (migrants, gay and lesbian communities, workers' alliances, etc.) that interrupt the presumed "naturalism" of the nation marked by an ideological codification of territory, of gender and of genealogy. According to Bhabha these minorities—who carry the marks of spatial histories of cultural dislocation—represent the "disjunctive" forms that make the nation above all a space of cultural circulation; or rather, those forms of discursive marginality which, turning to the "supplementary logic of secondariness" (ibid., 312), constantly negotiate strategic maneuvers of mediation *between* the ethnic, racial, and cultural boundaries.

A similar multiplication and production of differential spatialities and temporalities, diametrically opposed to the representation of the state–nation as "container" of the homogenous and unified space-temporality, is at the center of the fruitful analyses put forward by the theoretician and urbanist Saskia Sassen. In her own turn she brings to light the co-implications of mechanisms of exclusion and inclusion deriving from the interactive superimposition between "global" and "national" order: from the play between two "master/monster temporalities and spatialities" (Sassen 2001a, 276). The interaction between the "national" order and "global" order, indeed, rather than configuring itself as a zero-sum game in which one term loses meaning and pertinence at the expense of its other, gives rise to dynamic zones of intersection the results of which are characterized by a high level of unpredictability and variability: zones for which Sassen coins the notion of *analytic borderlands* (see Sassen 2006, 378 *et seqq.*). The usefulness of such a concept—claims the author in a monumental volume dedicated to the transformations of sovereignty in the global context—consists above all in "a heuristic device that allows one to take what is commonly represented as a line separating two differences, typically seen as mutually exclusive, into a conceptual field—a third entity—that requires its own empirical specification and theorization" (ibid., 379). In other words, Sassen records the emergence of specific "frontier zones" and "borderlands" that in configuring a new spatial–temporal order, pose new analytic challenges for the social sciences: both in terms of the activities and the subjects that characterize them and in terms of the theoretical and political instruments necessary to prevent their collapse into linear demarcations of difference. An instance of these *frontier zones*, albeit at a macro level, are the "global cities" in which there is the transformation of much of social space into a *border zone* (see Sassen 2001b; but on the explosion in much of the world of the urban fabric into an indistinct and chaotic "planet of slums," see Davis 2006; in Balibar 2007 we find instead a theoretical analysis centered on the French case of the *banlieues*). The global city tends, indeed, to be marked by operations of power and domination that elude the traditional codes of the political: whether they be the reticular and hyper-connected structure of the financial markets or the submerged exploitation of the migrant workforce. In this case the boundaries, far from being a space of social and cultural translation, are characterized as true and proper *states of exception* (or areas of "social death") excluded from all political or state control. States of exception that produce individuals *extra legem*, or, literally, *outlaws*: migrants, clandestines or refugees led—according to current lexis—to a condition of radically depoliticized "naked life" (see Agamben 2005) or, to borrow the words of Arjun Appadurai, to "an uneasy grey area between citizens proper and humanity in general" (Appadurai 2006, 42).

In Bhabha's words, the forked road between the border as a space of cultural translation and of liberation from the yoke of the nationalist and racial imaginary border is the site of a "struggle for the historical and ethical right to signify" (Bhabha 1995, 51). In traveling along this road, we must return to Balibar's fundamental analyses. Indeed Balibar has placed at the center of his own research on the contemporary transformation of political spaces the new statute of both the *heterogeneity* and of the *ubiquity* of borders: a statute by virtue of which if on the one hand in the new "areas of international transit"—those which Marc Augé has defined "non-places," or "globalized spaces of passage" (Augé 1992)—we witness a ferocious materialization of the *differential functioning* of the borders, which for some have the function of a real device of "internal exclusion," which of life creates a waiting-for-life, or a non-life; on the other hand it is no longer possible to "identify" borders according to a simply geographical, political, or administrative code given that borders are now dislocated and spread to wherever selective or security checks are in practice.[9] Nevertheless, Balibar has gone to greater depths to shed light on the matter (theoretical and historical) of the fact that around boundaries an entire conception of the *universal* and the *particular* has been and continues to be played out. This has come about through an effect of *symbolic surdetermination* (of doubling and of relativization together), meaning that the act itself of determining a boundary—national, racial, class-based or, we add, gender-based—sanctions at the same time a *configuration of the world*:

National borders would not be capable of securing (or trying to secure) *identities*, would not be capable of marking the threshold at which life and death are played out [. . .]; in brief—to take up the decisive formulation elaborated by Fichte in the *Addresses to the German Nation* (1897)—they would not be capable of being "internal borders" (internalized borders, borders for interiority) were they not idealized. And they would not be idealized, conceived of as the support of the universal, if they were not imagined as the point at which "worldviews," and thus also views of man, were at stake: the point at which one must choose, and choose *oneself*." (Balibar 2002, 94)

The *duplicity* of borders, the fact that they can institute and separate territories solely by structuring the universality of the world, and the fact that this *rise* (or this "doubling") is the condition of their becoming *internalized borders*, "borders for interiority," this is what leads back to—to borrow Balibar's words once again—the need for "a democratic radicalism which has as its aim to deconstruct the institution of the border" (ibid., 85). It is with regard to this need for a democratizing deconstruction of the "institution of the border" that it appears useful here to turn to that wealth of studies which, concentrating on the historical experiences of diaspora and the spatial and social dislocation of populations across the entire surface of the globe, has brought back into question the efficacy and the effectuality of the canonic and normative representation of state–nation modernity. Consider, as a fine example, the description provided by Paul Gilroy in *The Black Atlantic*: a space not only indelibly marked by the catastrophe and the violence of the so-called *middle passage* of the Black slave trade, but also reinvented and crossed again in the other direction by the Blacks themselves in a yearning for liberation irreducible to the "closed codes of *any* constricting or absolutist understanding of ethnicity." (Gilroy 1993, 138; but see also Linebaugh and Rediker 2000, and Mbembe 2006.) The "smooth space" of the Atlantic (furrowed by racial, national, and imperial boundaries as ferociously violent as they are apparently invisible) has indeed witnessed the rise of *cosmopolitic* cultures and practices which, by means of a constant crossing of boundaries and identities, have renewed the spatial–temporal coordinates of modern history, giving rise to "ecologies of belonging" located beyond all perimeters of identity (see Gilroy 2003, 19). The history of the African *diaspora*—moving away from a unidirectional, linear, and reversible model of dispersion: moving away, in other words, from any "myth of return"—thus gave rise to a sentiment of belonging rooted not so much in a form of immediate and essentialist pre-political fraternity, but rather in an eminently *social* experience characterized by devices of power exercised with violence on bodies "racialized" and subjected to processes of radical othering, or "alterization." In this sense, the cultural production of the Black diaspora—understood as a "counterculture" of modernity aiming at a redefinition of the canons of modern democracy—constitutes an example and an eminent historical instance of a cultural *ethos* lived as "nonessential essence," or as "nontraditional tradition": in other words, a model of *belonging* that is intrinsically *meta-ethnic* and, consequently, intimately *trans-national*. In naming this emerging form of belonging "translocal," Gilroy borrows the concept of "changing same" created by Amiri Baraka in his analysis of blues music: the "same that changes" here takes the guise of a historical memory rooted above all in a collective process of elaboration of suffering and in a dramaturgy of memory that "separates the genealogy from the geography and the dwelling from the belonging" (ibid., 31):

> As an alternative to the metaphysics of "race," of nation and of delimited territorial culture, all codified in the body, the diaspora is a concept that actively disturbs the cultural and historical workings of belonging. (ibid., p. 36)

"Diasporic nationalism" (or what Appadurai calls "delocalized transnation": Appadurai 1996, 172) thus configures a form of alternative loyalty with regard to the territorial codes of European nationalism and its boundaries, constituting itself rather as a figure of *trans-locality* in contrast with the processes of territorialization (and of normalization) of cultural identities. The diasporic consciousness, indeed, is the product not of an identity founded in affiliation to a territory, a language or a common ethnic group, but is a belonging that cannot be reduced to any rigid statutory perimetering rooted in historical memory and in the social dynamics of remembrance. It is along these lines that the figuration of the "diaspora"—as an experience of a radical suspension of identity—rises to become a symbolic cipher of a reconfiguration of the experience of *belonging* that indicates the creation of "transnational" practices that break the link between identity and territory: and this to the extent to which—to borrow Gilroy's words—"Dwelling in the interstices of mechanical solidarity reminds us how the concept of diaspora can offer real alternatives to the hard bond of primordial blood and the immediate pre-political brotherhood. The popular image of nations, races or natural ethnic groups spontaneously equipped with interchangeable collections of ordered bodies that express and reproduce absolutely distinctive cultures, is firmly rejected. [. . .] Once the simple sequence of explicative ties between place, location and consciousness is broken, it is also possible to throw into crisis the fundamental power of the territory in determining identity" (Gilroy 2003, 36).

2

Writing, Narrations

Is it up to the historian to take into account not only the damages, but also the wrong? Not only the reality, but also the meta-reality that is the destruction of reality? Not only the testimony, but also what is left of the testimony when it is destroyed (by dilemma), namely, the feeling? Not only the litigation, but also the differend? Yes, of course, if it is true that there would be no history without a differend, that a differend is born from a wrong and is signaled by a silence, that the silence indicates that phrases are in abeyance of their becoming event, that the feeling is the suffering of this abeyance.

—Jean-François Lyotard, *The Differend*

All these infinitely obscure lives remain to be recorded, I said [. . .] and went on in thought through the streets of London feeling in imagination the pressure of dumbness, the accumulation of unrecorded life.

—Virginia Woolf, *A Room of One's Own*

2.1. Counter-Histories

Since the publication of Said's *Orientalism* in 1978, colonial discourse analysis has concentrated prevalently on the "discursive operations" of colonialism: this is to say on the nexus—as submerged as it is materially active—that has tied language and historical–cultural forms of enquiry to the catastrophes of colonialism and imperialism. Said is almost the only one to place emphasis on the representation and discursive construction of alterity, but this has nevertheless been balanced over the years by a growing attention for the realities that this representation excluded or ignored: not only the suppressed voice of the "other," but also the "history of the subaltern," both in terms of the "objective" story of the subaltern or marginalized groups, and, following Frantz Franon, in terms of the "subjective" experience of the effects of colonialism and of domination. The most fruitful revisions of Said's seminal work have thus had the thorny question of the "representation" of alterity as their focus of enquiry, but through the mediation provided by an analysis of specific "counter-histories," focused on the unforeseen and unrepresented forms of subjectivity of the colonized subjects (see Young 1995, 159–61). To paraphrase Spivak, the Eurocentric strategies of imperialist "narrativization" of history were ever more decidedly accompanied by the production of "counter-narratives," the aim of which was above all to bring to light the "foreclosure" (the deletion from the dominant symbolic system) of the oppressed and colonized subject (Spivak 1999).[1] This is the case of the impressive theoretical and historiographical work undertaken from the 1980s onwards by the Indian historians of the Subaltern Studies Collective, whose primary objective was not only a widening of the "sources" for the historiographical practice and narration, but also a more general questioning of its hierarchies and its "traditional" stances. Their declared epistemological objective was to dismantle the elitist approach predominant in the official narrative of the achievement of independence from colonial domination on India's part. On the other hand the "subaltern studies" project, from its very inception with the words of its founder, Ranajit Guha, hinged on the problem of the "failure" (the "historical failure of the nation to come to its own") and therefore, in a move that was only apparently paradoxical, on the understanding of *a history that did not take place*. Guha wrote in the 1982 programmatic manifesto ("On Some Aspects of the Historiography of Colonial India"), which gave rise to the group's work:

> It is the study of this *historic failure of the nation to come to its own*, a failure due to the inadequacy of the bourgeoisie as well as of the working class to lead it into a decisive victory over colonialism and a bourgeois-democratic revolution of either the classic nineteenth-century type under the hegemony of the bourgeoisie or a more modern type under the hegemony of workers and peasants, that is a "new democracy"—*it is the study of this failure which constitutes the central problematic of the historiography of colonial India*. (Guha 1988b, 43)

The driving force of the work of the "subaltern historians" had consequently been the attempt to oppose the protocols of the nationalist historiography, Marxist and elitist, with a historiographical model that had as its focus those forms of subjectivity and revolt that—unanimously ignored by historians—constituted the blind spot of the official narratives regarding the construction of the Indian nation. In line with a movement whose genealogy has roots in British "history from below," in Black history and in "women's history" (see, for example, Traverso 2006, 22–24), the crucial epistemological objective here was not so much to add a mere "supplement" to monumental history, juxtaposing traditional historiography with a "history of the other" or "of the periphery," but rather to adopt as focus the writing and the forms of agency and subjectivity subjugated by the universalizing paradigms, following the need to recover suppressed histories, the experience of the "submerged" of World History, or the "heart of darkness" that the models of dominant discourse had not succeeded in penetrating. It is in this context that recourse to Gramsci's concept of "subaltern" acquires relevance (for more detail see below, part two, chapter 3, section 3.2.), understood as the "general attribute of subordination in South Asian society whether this is expressed in terms of class, caste, age, gender and office or in any other way." (Guha 1988a, 35.) If, nevertheless, as Gramsci wrote in his "Notes on Italian History," "The history of subaltern social groups is necessarily fragmented and episodic," it is precisely around notions such as "fragments," "traces" and "margins" that the attempt to rework the statute of the historical story revolves, as does the search for other and alternative narratives compared to the "imperial" narrative. Through an unprecedented attention for the "small voices" of subjects in revolt (Guha 1996) and a strategy of reading backwards in time, Guha turned particularly to the study of the "prose of the counter-insurrection" (colonial archives and sources), examining its "cuts, seams and stitches—those cobbling marks—which tell us about the material it is made of and the manner of its absorption into the fabric of writing" (Guha 1988c, 47). This in a search for an *other* presence as opposed to that of the elitist or colonial "I": a quest, we might say, for a series of "emerging" or "insurgent histories" (Prakash 1990, 401–03). As Gyanendra Pandey writes significantly on surveying the work of the group:

> The study of the fragment, or the voice from the edge, aims to uncover alternative viewpoints, the other perspectives and other ways of writing, to try and capture other perspectives. The 'fragment' in this usage is not just a 'bit'—the dictionary's 'piece broken off'—of a preconstituted whole. Rather, it is a disturbing element, a 'disturbance,' a contradiction shall we say, in the self-representation of that particular totality and those who uncritically uphold it.
>
> The fragment is, in this sense, an appeal to an alternative perspective, or at least the possibility of another perspective. It is a call to try and analyse the historical construction of the totalities we work with, the contradictions that survive within them, the possibilities they appear to fulfill, the dreams and possibilities apparently suppressed: in a word, the fragility and instability of the 'givens' (the 'meaningful totalities') of history. (Pandey 2000, 296)

In homage to this methodological line—centered on "voices," "omissions," and "interruptions"—Guha thus placed his stake on research, between the folds and the cracks of the narrative fabric, into the signs of the *autonomous experience* of the colonized as an effective "subject of rebellion" (Guha 1988c, 71), in contrast with the almost automatic classification as "History" of the events that had often played the role of commutator of Indian historiography into a "colonialist knowledge" entirely succumbed to the "code of counter-insurgency" (ibid., 70).

And nevertheless, from a similar historiographical project—aimed at recovering the "experience" and the "knowledge" of the subaltern and the dominated from the colonial archives—there inevitably arose contradictions relating to the epistemological protocols materially adopted and, above all, relating to the centrality granted to the category (of existential and phenomenological ilk) of "experience" (see, for example, O'Hanlon 2000). Indeed, is it truly possible, to write a *history* of oppression or of exploitation? Or, even better, is it possible to *make historical* that which was not *historical*? And, above all, is it possible to do this assuming that the *experience* of those whose "buried lives" one seeks to document is self-evident? In an important intervention regarding the creation of a paradigm aimed at formulating an alternative "women's history" of official history, the feminist historian Joan Scott was very effective in highlighting the aporias into which any project for a "history of difference" is destined to fall, whenever it is founded on the methodological assumption of the irreducibility and the autonomy of "experience": i.e., a referential notion of "evidence" as re-presentation of the real (Scott 1992; but see also Scott 1999). Indeed, not only does the appeal to experience reproduce the dominant ideological system according to which the facts "speak," but with this the "difference" finds itself neutralized and the "resistance" is collocated outside of its discursive frame: to the extent that, as Scott rightly recalls, "It is not individuals who have experience, but subjects who are constituted through experience" (Scott 1992, 25–26). If experience is thus an intimately "foundational" experience that inserts all attempts to historicize oppression within an ineluctably circular logic, then a "history of difference" cannot but tend inversely to configure itself as a *non-foundational history* or even as a "history without foundations." Indeed, it is with the term "*post-foundational* history" that the Subaltern Studies historian Gyan Prakash seeks to indicate that alternative to the "foundational" historical paradigm—the paradigm according to which every history is founded on some unique identity (individual, class, or structural) by which it is therefore representable; an identity that cannot be further disassembled into heterogeneous parts—centered on the study not of "essences," but of differences, which is to say of "relationships and processes that have constructed contingent and unstable identities." This is a web of "relations and practices" that leads to an acceptance of identities (historical, cultural, political) as *relational* rather than essential (see Prakash 1990, 399 *et seqq.*).

2.2. Archives of Silence

It will be useful at this point to examine the modes and the forms with which the considerations formulated above affect the protocols of historiographical practice and, specifically, the inscription and the formation of what we call "historical archive": meaning by this term not so much a mere warehouse of clues and documents, but rather the precipitate of specific instances (historical, social, institutional) of the production of knowledge that in itself is intrinsic to the operation of mechanisms and devices of power. Although the concept of "archive" has been magisterially fathomed and explored by Michel Foucault and by Michel de Certeau in particular (see Foucault 1972; de Certeau 1988; but see also Ricoeur 2004, 146 *et seqq.*), it is appropriate to dwell here on what Derrida wrote in this regard in a text dedicated to psychoanalytic and Freudian "archeology":

> In a way, the term indeed refers [. . .] to the *arkhē* in the *physical, historical,* or *ontological* sense, which is to say to the originary, the first, the principial, the primitive, in short to the commencement. But even more, and *even earlier,* "archive" refers to the *arkhē* in the *nomological*

sense, to the *arkhē* of the commandment. As is the case for the Latin *archivium* or *archium* [. . .] the meaning of "archive," its only meaning, comes to it from the Greek *arkheion*: initially a house, a domicile, an address, the residence of the superior magistrates, the *archons*, those who commanded. [. . .] With such a status, the documents, which are not always discursive writings, are only kept and classified under the title of the archive by virtue of a privileged *topology*. They inhabit this unusual place, this place of election where law and singularity intersect in *privilege*. At the intersection of the topological and the nomological, of the place and the law, of the substrate and the authority, a scene of domiciliation becomes at once visible and invisible. (Derrida 1995, 9–10)

Thus there is a *violence* of the archive, a violence as archive, or an "archival violence" (ibid., 12), through which power acquires control of memory and the monopoly of the political as *res publica* and "common thing." Along analogous lines, in an important article dedicated to Western historiography's suppression and obliteration of the revolution of Haitian slaves in 1791 (the first victorious revolution of slaves who thus vindicated the universality of Jacobin principles against their very promulgators), the Haitian historian Michel-Rolph Trouillot has significantly brought attention to the specific operations of devices of power that function by rendering each historical narrative nothing less than a "particular bundle of silences" (Trouillot 1995, p. 27). Devices that operate above all by means of well-determined strategies of occultation and silencing: where "silence" is "an active and transitive process: one 'silences' a fact or an individual as a silencer silences a gun" (ibid., 48):

> Silences are inherent in history because any single event enters history with some of its constituting parts missing. Something is always left out while something else is recorded. There is no perfect closure of any event, however one chooses to define the boundaries of that

> event. Thus whatever becomes fact does so with its own inborn absences, specific to its production. In other words, the very mechanisms that make any historical recording possible also ensure that historical facts are not created equal. They reflect differential control of the means of historical production at the very first engraving that transforms an event into a fact. (ibid., 49)

The revision of the canons of historiographical writing is thus configured as a "battleground for historical power" (ibid.) where what is in question is the very conception of history as an institutionalized presentation of the past: a history that stands on "realism" as a privileged mode of narration and, therefore, also stands on protocols that are centered on the subject of an abstract and universalizing humanism. What is at stake here particularly is the category of "historical evidence," i.e., the identification of that which can be adopted as "proof" of historical truth. This implies an entire conception of what has value as "reality" (but regarding the question of what has value as "proof" in historiography and, in particular, regarding the relationships between "historical truth," "proof," and "rhetoric," see Ginzburg 2000). In his day Jean-François Lyotard had already remarked on the strictly "protocol" conception of the identification of the reality status of an event (a conception intimately linked to a *serial* model of temporality), defining it as "totalitarian in its principle" and setting against it a *recursive* narrative model (Lyotard 1988, 5). Nevertheless, unlike some products of what is called the postmodern, postcolonial criticism—bringing into discussion the fundamental nexus between historicism, realism and empiricism—does not draw a merely "literary" or "narratological" vision from historiography, but rather an intimately *political* rereading of the relationships between historiographical practice and historical reality: to the extent that the principal focus of the enquiry, and the unavoidable field of study, continues to reside in the analysis of the structures of *dominion* and *subordination* (see, for example, Prakash 1990, 400–01).

From this point of view it is particularly the excavation work of Dipesh Chakrabarty that provides us with an acute bringing into focus of the contradictions that have tormented the various attempts at *writing* a "history of the subaltern." Evidence of this is the fact that, after having identified in a "romantic–populist" root the wellspring of the aporias in Guha's original project, a project that had led him to superimpose an "experience" (and a "consciousness") already formed for a battlefield on the very forms of subjectivity of the subaltern, the Indian historian embarks on a fruitful comparison with the perspectives of Hayden White (see Chakrabarty 2004). Indeed, in a famous essay titled, "The Politics of Historical Interpretation: Discipline and De-Sublimation" (1982), White had brought into focus a movement of "disciplining" of historiographical practice (a movement toward transformation of historiography into a codified "discipline") that coincided totally with a series of *denials* and *exclusions* (only apparently "stylistic") full of consequences regarding the *type of events* that can be narrated historically (see White 1987). More specifically, White recorded a yielding of historiographical writing to an essentially "deliberative" model of discourse (founded on the "rule of evidence") from which—in the historian's view—there descended a form of "political domestication of historical facts":

> For both the Left and the Right, this same aesthetics of the beautiful presides over the process in which historical studies are constituted as an autonomous scholarly discipline. [. . .] For this tradition, whatever "confusion" is displayed by the historical record is only a surface phenomenon: a product of lacunae in the documentary sources, of mistakes in ordering the archives, or of previous inattention or scholarly errors. If this confusion is not reducible to the kind of order that a science of laws might impose upon it, it can still be dispelled by historians endowed with the proper kind of understanding. (White 1987, 70–77)

The "disciplinary" aspects of history thus regard researching the "beautiful" that *politically domesticates* historical facts, preventing them from showing their own "sublime" face: and here, according to White, the "sublime" corresponds to an *innate resistance to order on the part of history*. Moreover, the imputation of a meaning that "politically domesticates" history according to the canons of an aesthetic of the "beautiful" sits neatly with a conception of historical explanation as, literally, *production of order*. It is nevertheless precisely in that nexus between the "disciplining" of historiography and the production of an "ordered" reality that Chakrabarty rightly identifies the juncture between hegemonic and Eurocentric historiography and categories derived from (or strictly related to) modern political philosophy. If it is true, as Foucault maintained in *Surveiller et punir* (1975), that the first among the great operations of "discipline" is the production of "*tableaux vivants*," of "ordered" multiplicity (according to the injunction of the disciplinary practice that *identifies to control*), then the empirical–individualist method, or rather, the methodological individualism characteristic of those forms of history that obey, according to White's formula, an aesthetic of the "beautiful," aligns the historiographical discipline with the disciplinary and normalizing practices of the state, revealing a non-contingent but constitutive nexus between the individualizing procedure of hegemonic historiography and the Hobbesian myth of sovereignty (see Chakrabarty 2004, 247). In *Les Mots de l'histoire* (1992) Jacques Rancière—referenced by Chakrabarty himself—defined this "alliance between the point of view of science and that of the royal place" as "royal-empiricism" (Rancière 1994, 21): an alliance by virtue of which not only is there an elimination of the homonymy that torments the term "history" ("event" and "story," or *Geschichte* and *Historie*), but the very "axes" of time are flattened on a simultaneous "realist" present:

> Every event, among speakers, is tied to an excess of speech in the specific form of a displacement of the *statement*: an appropriation "outside the truth" of the speech of the other (of the formulas of sovereignty, of

the ancient text, of the sacred word) that makes it signify differently [. . .]. The event draws its paradoxical novelty from that which is tied to something restated, to something stated out of context, inappropriately. The impropriety of expression is also an undue superimposition of time periods. The event has the novelty of the anachronistic. And the revolution, which is the event par excellence, is par excellence the place where social science is constituted in the denunciation of the impropriety of the words and of the anachronism of the events. [. . .] The original ghost of social science is the revolution as anachronism [. . .] Royal-empiricist analysis [. . .] proceeds in the other direction, on the temporal axis, by the conjoint disqualification of the categories of past and future. The utopia that guides its interpretations is that of a science whose categories would be adequate to their object because they would be exactly contemporaneous with it. The present is its time. (Rancière 1994, 30–31)

Against this "royal-empiricist" model, Rancière examines the revolution of the *Annales*, which gave rise to the passage from the history of kings to the history of the seas, of the spaces of "civilization," of the *longue durée* and the life of the anonymous: a history which, having pushed to the limit the indeterminacy of the referent, recovers its own character as "mixed discourse" that *semanticizes* and *narrativizes at the same time*. Even more, Rancière—and with him Chakrabarty—set up against the violence of the documents and the "methodological individualism of the police and the court of law" (Chakrabarty 2004, 247) "forms of knowledge proper to the age of the masses" (Rancière 1994, 23), which (again dissolving the distinction between *story* and *history*, or between *Historie* and *Geschichte*) knows how to produce "counter-histories" in which the life of the subaltern is inscribed, or, in Rancière's expression, the "excess of words" is out of place. But it goes without saying that a discourse which is able to accept the "aleatory subjectivization" of de-essentialized singularities and "places of speech that are not designatable localities but rather singular articulations between the order of speech and that of classifications" (ibid., 92) cannot but radically question once again the very statute of historical temporality (its modalizations, and the function of the "possible" in history) on which the (fallacious) representation of the *continuum* at the basis of monumental history is founded.

2.3. Narratives of the Possible

We have seen how, within the framework of postcolonial criticism, the attempt to disarticulate the Orientalist and imperial "continuity" was played out above all around the effort to rethink the coordinates of historical representation. This began from a revisitation (post-Foucauldian) of the requirements of the "archive" and of that which once had value as "proof" within historiographical narration, to the point of the declared need to instigate "counter-histories" that unhinge from within the sequential order on which the hegemony of a well-determined concept (unilinear and cumulative) of temporal processes is founded. It is useful here to note how a similar call for the production of "counter-histories" was put into action, following coordinates that were in part analogous, and in the same temporal arc, of what is known as New Historicism (whose major theoretician and exponent is Stephen Greenblatt). This, in a quest for a compromise between the deconstructionist radicalism of textual politics and traditional humanism, sought to configure itself as a *history of the possibilities* that emerge on the surface of "representation" through the singular voices and the idiosyncratic visions to be found in the midst of the weave of the historical text (see Gallagher and Greenblatt 2000). In particular, gaining leverage on *parallel histories* (such as the history of the human body, the history of aesthetic motives or of forms of discourse), New Historicism set up against the continuous History of the dominant tradition a form of "counter-history," the aim of which was to bring to the surface and render apparent "the slippages, cracks, fault lines, and surprising absences in the monumental structures that dominated a more traditional historicism" (ibid., 17). In this attempt to delineate a "history of the possibilities of history" the strategic use of the *petit récit* and the anecdote acquires relevance in the disarticulation of the historical *continuum* and at the same time the revelation of its excesses. In *Marvelous Possessions: The Wonder of the New World* (1991), for example, Greenblatt, recording the passage from Medieval wonder as a mode of dispossession to Renaissance wonder as a drive toward appropriation and "colonization of the marvelous," had already played the *petites histoires* (bearers of a "shock of the unfamiliar" and a "local excitement of discontinuous wonders") against the *grand récit* of integrated and progressive history, demonstrating how historical discourse was constantly interrupted by *lapsus* and affirmed that "If anecdotes are registers of the singularity of the contingent—associated [. . .] with the rim rather than the immobile and immobilizing center—they are at the same time recorded as *representative* anecdotes" (Greenblatt 1991, 3). On the theoretical plane, the use of the anecdotal dimension sits at the point of intersection between the requirements of the British "history from below" and a recovery of Foucault as paradigm of the *pathos* of historical anecdotes. Nevertheless, if in British radical history the challenge to the unidirectional *continuum* at the foundation of both liberal historiography and Marxist determinism had been conducted by means of a declared attention for "experience," for "consciousness," i.e., for the "world-making" of lived experience (one thinks in particular of Edward Palmer Thompson's work), New Historicism sought leverage on the Foucauldian method in order to shatter the *continuum* of the "big stories." Indeed, through this method the anecdote appears in its nature as *residue*, or, better, as the *precipitate* of the ceaseless struggle carried out against the disciplining and normalizing power materialized in the historical archive (see Gallagher and Greenblatt 2000, 49–73). Consider, for example, that extraordinary and very dense text that is *La Vie des homes infâmes* (1977), in which Foucault not only offered a "herbarium of singular lives," excluded from the canvas of history, but also allowed the emergence of scene in which a power awaits at the breach, persecutes and, in this way, *identifies* infamous and vile existences:

> In order that something of this should come across even to us, it was nevertheless necessary that a beam of light should, at least for a moment, illuminate them. A light which comes from somewhere else. What rescues them from the darkness of night where they would, and still should perhaps, have been able to remain, is an encounter with power: without this collision, doubtless there would no longer be a single word to recall their fleeting passage. [. . .] All these lives, which were destined to pass beneath all discourse and to disappear without ever being spoken, have only been able to leave behind traces—brief, incisive and often enigmatic—at the point of their instantaneous contact with power. (Foucault 1979, 79–80)

What was Foucault suggesting in these few lines? That the "white gaze" of power paradoxically preserves subjects in the very act of destroying them; that his "momentary beam of light" renders one's Other visible (the abject, the excluded from History). Yes, it destroys the Other, but at the same time "petrifies" the Other, in such a way that *another history* takes shape as an eternal "landscape of ruins" (but for a criticism of this Foucauldian model of a culture that does not exist outside of the gesture of that which suppresses it, see the celebrated introduction to Carlo Ginzburg's *The Cheese and the Worms* in which he ungenerously accuses Foucault of "aestheticizing irrationality" and, even more, of "populism with its symbols reversed. A 'black' populism—but populism just the same" (Ginzburg 1980, xviii). In this sense the lure of anecdotal power fielded by New Historicism operates as a reference to a history freed of all teleologism: a history that is the *history of the possibilities of history*, the history of "historical virtuality" or, again, "the history of that which could have happened." Such a radical *pluralization of the past*, according to which the anecdote interrupts the historical *continuum*, revealing "the fingerprints of the accidental, suppressed, defeated, uncanny, abjected or exotic" (Gallagher and Greenblatt 2000, 52) points therefore not to the linear dynamic of a single possible historical economy, but to the structure of an alternative economy that questions in the most fundamental manner the confines between modes of narration.

And nevertheless, already on the plane of its theoretical background, New Historicism presents some glaring aporias. On the one hand, indeed, the anecdotal approach to historical and more generally cultural texts risks collusion with an intimately "modernist" form of "collecting": wherein, as James Clifford highlights in a famous and evocative essay dedicated to the relationship between anthropology and surrealism, each "collection" always implies a *metahistory* that "defines which groups or things will be redeemed from a disintegrating human past and which will be defined as the dynamic, or tragic, agents of a common destiny" (Clifford 1988, 13; but more generally see 215–52). The anecdotal and "collector's" forms of cultural description, argues Clifford, are in truth inextricably linked "to obsession, to reminiscence," thus continuing the purely "modernist" tradition of an acquisitive subjectivity that obtains leverage on a constant *reification* of the past, redeemed as an atemporal "origin." On the other hand, despite the abandonment of a "continuist" model, hinging on the assumption of a substantial cumulativity of historical process, in favor instead of a conception focalized on its ruptures and dislocations, there remains in New Historicism the adhesion to the presupposition that there is nothing "either side of history": nothing that is not in the true sense *historicizable*. But it is precisely a similar denial of the possibility of a *nucleus of resistance* to the historicizing narrative—of the possibility that something *always* remains unarticulated in every historical plot—that leads New Historicism to isolate each historical moment from that which precedes it and from that which follows it, and to reduce it tautologically to the *mere contemporaneity with itself.*

We have seen vice versa how the field of postcolonial studies, centered on a fierce criticism of the very category of "contemporaneity," has instead called into question any and all forms of "naturalism" of historical time—wherein, by "naturalism" one means the theoretical–practical conviction that *everything* is always completely *historicizable*—setting up as an issue the phenomenon of suppression of the fundamental *an-achrony* (if not "a-chrony") that inhabits historical time, and consequently bringing out the paradoxical "anachronistic" logic of the revolutionary and/or anticolonial movements.[2] It has been written—in the wake of the previously cited Rancière—that the historian cannot but take the anachronism into account, that "other time" which is "that time that one experiences when time is, in a very Shakespearian way, 'unhinged,' that other time that must in any case be postulated, if for no other reason than to give a status to all that which, in an epoch, one thinks before it, on the mode of anticipation" (Loraux 1993, 23–24): to everything, therefore, that relates to *repetition*.[3] As has been mentioned, an analogous theoretical imperative governs postcolonial criticism: this by the extent to which subaltern pasts are "pasts that resist historicization" (Chakrabarty 2000, 101), setting out the epistemological limits of every "historicism." Operating as "supplements" to the historical past, they are "signposts of this border" (ibid., 110), bringing to light a fundamental non-contemporaneity of the present with itself, which lacerates the seriality of historical time and simultaneously refers to the *double bind* that weaves present and past together, beyond any academic or disciplinary discourse on historiography.

3

Aporias of Memory

> The sight of the ruins leads us to intuit fleetingly the existence of a time that is not the time the history books speak of, or which the restorers seek to bring back to life. It is a *pure* time, not datable, absent from this our world of images, of simulacra and reconstructions, absent from this violent world of ours in which rubble no longer has time to become ruins.
>
> —Marc Augé, *Le temps en ruines*

3.1. The Law of the Past: Ruins and Other Remains

Postcolonial criticism in the "historicist" matrix of European historical and political thought is not resolved in a simple liquidation of the problem of historicization. Indeed, the relationship between "subaltern pasts" and historicization is not at all configured as a relationship of mutual exclusion, but rather calls attention to a field of tension generated by multiple intersections between past, present, and future, which stymies any and all linear and progressive visions of historical time. In describing Caribbean history—a history of populations who were violently robbed and had their own historicity expropriated—Édouard Glissant comes to conceive of the past in "prophetic" terms, like a past still clinging to and melded with the present, a past whose image the theoretician and the writer must constantly seek to grasp:

> The past, to which we were subjected, which has not yet emerged as history for us, is, however, obsessively present. The duty of the writer is to explore this obsession, to show its relevance in a continuous fashion to the immediate present. This exploration is therefore related neither to a schematic chronology nor to a nostalgic lament. It leads to the identification of a painful notion of time and its full projection forward into the future, without the help of those plateaus in time from which the West has benefitted, without the help of that collective density that is the primary value of an ancestral cultural heartland. That is what I call *a prophetic vision of the past*. (Glissant, 1989, 64)

A similar "prophetic vision of the past"—for which the past is obsession and projection toward the future at the same time—sits perfectly with a conception of history as constitutively "unfinished," or, to turn back to Walter Benjamin, *unabgeschlossene*. Reference to the Benjamin of the *Über den Begriff der Geschichte* theses is, after all, persistent and crucial in much of postcolonial criticism.[1] And this not only because of the corrosive criticism aimed at the concept of "progress" (*Fortschritt*) and at what is necessarily correlated, i.e., the idea that history proceeds "through a homogeneous, empty time" (Benjamin 2003, 395). But also because of the radical overturning of the "axes" of time applied there, by virtue of which it is the past that rises to *terminus ad quem* of the historical yearning for liberation. In the celebrated "Thesis II," after having affirmed that each past "carries a secret index with it, by which it is referred to redemption," Benjamin indeed asked himself, "Doesn't a breath of the air that pervaded earlier days caress us as well? In the voices we hear, isn't there an echo of now silent ones?" (ibid., 390). The voices suffocated and silenced in the story of the continuity of the winners mark here an original *law of the past*, constantly renewed by "a secret agreement between past generations and the present one" (ibid.). The *Erlösung*, or redemption, thus takes the form not of a mere historical recollection of the victims of the past, but a fulfillment, on the part of the present, of that which *could have been* but *has not been*: a *restitutio ad integrum* or a *restitutio omnium* that is at the same time a *novum*.[2] Benjamin's image of history as a *critical constellation* that a particular fragment of the past forms specifically with a particular moment in the present, thus opening itself up to "redemption," belongs entirely to postcolonial criticism: the present, crossing itself with the "past" (*Vergangenheit*) converts itself into the "moment" (*Augenblick*)—or rather, into the radical and democratic "now" of which Chakrabarty speaks—not already by virtue of a Utopian drive toward the future, but because of the flashes of the image of an *uncompensated past* of the oppressed, of the victims and those with no name.[3] The power and the topical nature of Benjamin's theses from a postcolonial point of view therefore reside in a radical *re-opening of the past*, centered on an awareness that the historical variant that has triumphed is not the only possible one; that the historicist and quantitative concept of time as "accumulation" has opposition in a time that is qualitative, heterogeneous and full: a "tradition of the oppressed" that is radically *discontinuous* (in his preparatory "Notes" to the "Theses" Benjamin wrote, "The history of the oppressed is a *discontinuum* [. . .] The *continuum* of history is that of the oppressors. While the idea of the *continuum* razes everything to the ground, the idea of the *discontinuum* is the foundation of true tradition." (See Benjamin 1979b, 1236, but on the concept of "tradition" in Benjamin, see above all Arendt 1968) This "true tradition" is woven into the course of the succession of historical forms of domination and of oppression. The past from the point of view of the oppressed is not indeed the cumulative *continuum* of conquests, but is an interminable series of "interruptions," of "failures." In a suggestive reading of the *Theses on the Concept of History*, Eric Santner has identified in these failures some "symptoms" that *press* on the present, reconfiguring democratic and revolutionary action as an action directed toward repeating/redeeming the failed attempts of the past:

> [Symptoms] are not so much forgotten deeds, but rather forgotten *failures* to act, failures to *suspend* the

force of social bond inhibiting acts of solidarity with society's "others." Symptoms register not only past failed revolutionary attempts but, more modestly, past *failures to respond* to calls for action or even for empathy on behalf of those whose suffering in some sense belongs to the form of life of which one is a part. They hold the place of something that is *there*, that *insists* in our life, though it has never achieved full ontological consistency. Symptoms are thus in some sense the virtual archives of *voids*—or, perhaps, better, defenses against voids—that persist in historical experience. (quoted in Žižek 2002, 255)

Here, as we have seen, sits the inextricable link that pulls postcolonialism and anticolonialism together: in the profound sense that the historical *failure* of the latter acquires, in its being together an archive of "lacunae" and a "symptom that presses" on the present (see Mezzadra and Rahola 2015; but on the close-knit relationship between anticolonialism and postcolonialism see, in general, Young 2001). From this point of view, history becomes not only a "partial" history (in that it is dictated by the "constellation" that is on each occasion unique as it forms at the meeting between past and present), but also a "partisan" history: a *critical history* which, aiming at a redemption of the past, is configured first and foremost as a *soteriology*. To pick up on the words of the Italian scholar Enzo Melandri, who works in exploring the theoretical depth of field of the category (at once both Freudian and Foucauldian) of "archeology":

> 'critical history' certainly cannot be resolved by pure and simple historiographical methodology. It must trace back the real genealogy of the events it studies. The division that has come to be established between historiography (*historia rerum gestarum*) and real history (*res gestae*) is very similar to that which has always existed between conscious and unconscious in Freud's

view. So critical history has the function of a therapy the aim of which is the recovery of the unconscious as historical "suppression" [. . .] Thus this is a *regression*: not, however, to the unconscious as such, but rather to that which has made it unconscious—in the dynamic sense of suppressed. [. . .] Understood thus, the concept of regression becomes so wide as to include within its virtual jurisdiction not only Mozart's *Don Giovanni* or Freud's *Traumdeutung*, but also the Black Power movement and every other emergence of the suppressed, the excluded and the alienated. History, therefore, can call itself critical only to the extent to which it is recovery of the alienated, of the excluded and of the suppressed. (Melandri 2004, 65–67)

The "non-rationalizing regression" of which *critical history* consists, in Melandri's words, therefore has as its own object and term the "history of something that did not happen," analogous to what happens in the historical–critical project of "subaltern studies." It, in other terms, is yes a *soteriology*, but it is also at the same time a *ruinology* regressing into the past with one's gaze turned to the future: a powerful symbolic inversion of the figure of Benjamin's angel of history. Thus conceived, history appears as an allegorical construct that exposes the *ruins of time*. In these ruins, as Dipesh Chakrabarty writes in an essay with the significant title "After History," when dealing with the question of what comes after history it must be remembered not only that history rises on the *ruins* of other forms of past, but also that those pasts "die" when their objects begin to appear as mere remains or spoils (see Chakrabarty 2005). If it is true that the ruins are not the simple result of a subtraction, of a consumption, but they themselves carry the trace of forms that are in perpetual evolution in response to the gaze that falls on them, it is equally true that they represent the mark of a time that escapes or resists History—the historicizing drive of a temporal movement that swallows and erases the past, absorbing it into a homogeneous and undifferentiated dimension. Indeed, a similar "ruinological" and "stratigraphic" paradigm of historical time had already been evocatively suggested by Claude Lévi-Strauss precisely in relation to the approach of Western ethnography with regard to the "other" times and places it would meet. In *Tristes Tropiques* he found himself affirming that as an "archaeologist of space" he was forced to "repiece together the idea of the exotic with the help of a particle here and a fragment of debris there" (Lévi-Strauss 1961, 44). But the analogy between time and ruins is not explored much beyond this in the text, indicating a dimension of time that *resists* all historicizing drive and at the same time gives rise to a temporal economy whose physiognomy must still be researched:

> Forgetfulness has done its work among my recollections, but it has not merely worn them thin, not merely buried them. It has made of these fragments a construction in depth that offers firmer ground beneath the feet and a clearer outline for the eye. One order has been substituted for another. Two cliffs mark the distance between my eye and its object; in the middle ground Time, which eats away at those cliffs, has begun to heap up the debris. The high ridges begin to fall away, piece by considerable piece; Time and Place come into opposition, blend oddly with one another, or become reversed, like sediment shaken clear by the trembling of a withered skin. Sometimes an ancient and infinitesimal detail will come away like a whole headland; and sometimes a complete layer of my past will vanish without trace. Unrelated events, rooted in the most disparate of regions and periods, suddenly come into contact with one another and take shape as a crusader castle which owes its architecture not to my private history but to some altogether wiser designer. (Lévi-Strauss 1961, 45)

But it goes without saying that a "ruinological" paradigm such as this—centered on awareness of the pasts' "capacity for dying" and of the drive to recover their outline and that which in them *was* seeking liberation—inevitably implies considerable consequences regarding the question (political and methodological) of the *writing* of history.

3.2. Historical Sublime and Narrative

We have seen how the relationship of intersection and of mutual and irreducible co-implication between the modalizations of time crystalized in the dimensions of the present, the past and the future, assumes—within the outline of a postcolonial criticism that has taken up and re-elaborated Benjamin's famous revision of European and Western "historicist" culture—a radically political profile. Here it becomes an instrument for rethinking the axis of "liberation" as a rejoining between the experience of the victims of the past and the action of those who "decide" to take on the load of that suffering and oppression according to the urgency of today or of the current situation. It is useful now to return to the debate on historiographical practice and in particular that part of it regarding the "writing" of history: a history that "did not happen" or, better, a history "without witnesses" (regarding the category of "events without witnesses," elaborated in relation to the catastrophes of the twentieth century, and, more specifically, in relation to the repercussions of a history that in its essence is "not over," a history the consequences of which are in perpetual evolution, see Felman and Laub 1992). In this context, it is again Dipesh Chakrabarty who offers a useful line of analysis, wherein—examining opportunities and aporias of the writing of a "history of the subaltern"—he refers to Hayden White's notion of "historical sublime": i.e., the idea of an innate *confusion* in history (or of an innate resistance of history to order), irrecoverable except from beginning with rhetorical and narratological models that in their turn refer to underlying political and ideological choices (but on the ideological and "meta-historical" dimension which, irreducible in every historical summary, would make a model of "rhetorical" analysis essential, the canonical reference is to White 1973). Chakrabarty picks up this category of "historical sublime," declining it within the need to write a history of the oppressed and the subaltern as its point of departure, and consequently asking himself: "If historical processes are indeed characterized by what White calls 'confusion,' then if one does not wish simply to domesticate this 'incomprehensible' aspect of history by making it all look orderly and ordered, how would one go about representing the unrepresentable, i.e., the sublime?" (Chakrabarty 2004, 236). In order to understand what is at stake here, it is useful nevertheless to give some attention to the context in which White develops, and in part revises, the radically "narratological" and "constructivist" position elaborated in his most famous text, *Metahistory* (1973), in which the only modality for constructing and discriminating between historical summaries corresponds to a criterion of "effective narration." Indeed, the idea of "historical sublime" does introduce us to the methodological question of the "writing" of history (with the related aporias tied to the problem of the "referentiality" of the historical discourse), but it refers even more to the problem of the historicization of traumatic events and of the historiographical modalities of writing on trauma (of which the Holocaust is, evidently, a paradigmatic example and a primary object of study): a problem, therefore, that inevitably torments White's exquisitely tropological and rhetorical approach.

In his important 1992 essay, "Historical Emplotment and the Problem of Truth," White deals with the aporias of his own tropological model beginning with the idea of "absolute limits" placed on historical representation regarding a certain class of traumatic events that are particularly intractable for a conventional historiographical instrumentation, be it positivist or constructivist. White's essay in truth sits in the context of a *querelle* that was acted out on American soil regarding the notion of the "limits of representation," a notion that lends itself to the title of an important volume edited by the historian Saul Friedlander, *Probing the Limits of Representation*, which provides an account of a meeting held in 1989 on the notion of "historical truth" involving such scholars as, indeed, Hayden White and Carlo Ginzburg (see Friedlander, ed.

1992). The lines of discussion elaborated there gravitated around the idea of "limits of representation," which is to say around the problem of the prerequisites for the representability of extreme events and the capacity of the canonical forms of historiography to accommodate traumatic historical experiences such as the "final solution." As shown by Paul Ricoeur, in this context the category of "limit of representation" should be declined in two different registers: since it is both an *external* limit, concerning the depletion of the available forms of representation in our culture, and an *internal* limit of a "need to recount" that rises from the very heart of the events themselves and forbids, "any sojourn in the land of semiotics." (Ricoeur 2004, 254.) From this debate onwards a variety of positions unfolded, bringing into question the canons of historiographical writing, whether it be conceived according to a positivist–documentary protocol or within the rhetorical–constructivist paradigm. From our point of view here, however, it is useful to dwell on White's above-mentioned essay, taken up and fully assimilated by Chakrabarty. In it White, turning to Roland Barthes's famous, "To Write: an Intransitive Verb?," indeed invokes an "analogous discursive" of the ancient "middle voice" as a modality of writing of the experiences of the victims that is neither subjective nor objective, but is objective–subjective (see White 1992, 47 *et seqq.*). This occurs because the "middle voice" is a voice that is neither active (subject) nor passive (object) and, consequently, it tends to mitigate, in White's opinion, the subject/object dichotomy that characterizes the disciplinary "realism" of historical prose, pointing rather to a relation of *mutual immanence* between agent and action, discourse and referent: i.e., to a dimension that is antecedent to the distinction between agent and patient, subjectivity and objectivity, fact and fiction, history and myth. In this way, the "middle voice" has a role in Derrida's *différance*, resisting all binary oppositions and configuring itself as the *"in-between* voice" of the unavailability and ambivalence of every position. Nevertheless, as has been shown with crystal clarity by the United States historian Dominick LaCapra, White's important essay presents glaring aporias. Indeed, LaCapra not only highlights how the debate generated by the interrogative on the requirements of historical "representability" of the Holocaust raises, in an accentuated form, problems that crop up with regard to other series of extreme and traumatic events that are "highly cathected" (see LaCapra 2001): in the face, in other words, of the "Holocausts of the others" (see Davis 2001). But he also turns his gaze on the *transferal* dimension of the relationship with the past (which is to say on the constituent implication of the present of the historian in his own object of study), refuted both by documentary and constructivist approaches. Thus the proposal—accepted by Ricoeur himself—of applying the psychoanalytic pair of "acting out" and "working-through" (corresponding to the Freudian dyad, formulated in the 1914 essay, "Remembering, Repeating and Working-through," of *Wiederholung* and *Durcharbeitung*: see Freud 1914) in understanding the dynamics of historiographical writing.[4] From this point of view, White's essay appears symptomatic of an *impasse* into which much of contemporary thought falls, whereby the insistence on the undecidability and *différance*, aporias and double binds, appears as the only guarantee of the absence of metaphysical totalization and of closure of history and of the subject. If it is true, indeed, that "there is a sense in which transference indicates that one begins inquiry in a middle-voiced 'position,'" undecidability and *différance*, threatening to disarticulate relations, to confuse the self and the other, and to make all distinction collapse, "are related to transference and prevail in trauma and in post-traumatic acting out in which one is haunted or possessed by the past and performatively caught up in the compulsive repetition of traumatic scenes—scenes in which the past returns and the future is blocked or fatalistically caught up in a melancholic feedback loop." (LaCapra 2001, 36 and 21.) Consider, for example, the later Derrida's insistence on the themes of "spectrality" and "impossible mourning," on the necessity of a logic of the *hantise* or a generalized *hantologie* (see Derrida 2002), for which the return of the past takes the form of "haunting" (*hantise*), of repetition, of an instability of time which, throwing temporal modes into blurriness, does no more than continually destabilize the present. But if in the acting-out, in the *constraint-*

to-repeat, each duality or double inscription of time in the past and future collapses, producing aporias and double binds, it is precisely in the insistence on the undecidability and ambivalence—of which White has been a supporter on the historiographic plane—that it is possible to discern a "mythical structure" which links itself to a practice of "melancholic repetition," an "acting-out" by virtue of which the "historical trauma" is converted, according to a formula of dislocated sacrality, for the occasion into the "sublime."

Set against the concept centered on the radical ambivalence of each position—or on the "undecidability" of a "middle voice" of history—is a vision of the historical past as the scene of losses that can be *narrated*: where the process of working through (the Freudian *Trauerarbeit*, or the "re-elaboration") implies above all a practice of "translation" and of "figuration" of the loss. From this point of view typically "postcolonial" practices acquire relevance, such as the Latin American *testimonio* and the various commissions on truth and reconciliation instituted over the last thirty years in Latin America, Africa, and South Africa. The practice of the *testimonio*—associated almost exclusively with Latin America and at the center of an extended debate beginning from the 1980s—consists of the recording and transcription of an *oral recount* of violence and oppression by an external interlocutor—a writer, activist, or journalist (see Beverley 1989, and Beverley and Zimmerman 1990). If "testimony" in Western societies is a calque on a legal model, here on the contrary there is a radical problematization of the distinction between history and literature that reconfigures the very notion of "truth" in the representation, constituting a sort of "zone of indeterminacy" that shatters the compartmentalization between genres of discourse. The primary objective of a practice such as the *testimonio* is in fact the construction of an *intimidad pública* and, above all, a collective subject of the discourse that takes charge of a common narrative. Consider the famous opening of *I, Rigoberta Menchú* ("Me llamo Rigoberta Menchú y asi me nació la conciencia") by the Guatemalan Rigoberta Menchú (winner, in 1992, of the Nobel Peace Prize): "My name is Rigoberta Menchú. I am twenty three years old. This is my testimony. I didn't learn it from a book and I didn't learn it alone. I'd like to stress that it's not only *my* life, it's also the testimony of my people." (Menchú 1984, 1.) This affirmation of a self-identity that is inseparable from the collective identity of the oppressed group as the modality through which the "historical truth" of oppression can be testified, is at the basis of those discursive forms of public re-working of a collective memory that are the various commissions on truth and reconciliation. In particular, the celebrated South African Truth and Reconciliation Commission, instigated by Nelson Mandela and chaired by Archbishop Desmond Tutu from 1996 to 1998, hinged on the attempt to define a "transitional justice" on the basis of a "politics of memory" which, through the re-elaboration of what in another context Primo Levi defined as "unnecessary violence," would be able to establish a new correspondence between reality and the violence of the past and belonging to a present that must take on the burden of that past. In this case, as has been underlined by Eva Hoffmann, the *performative* gesture of memory and public recognition had as their specific objective a form of *symbolic redirectioning*, able to establish a "metaphorical demarcator" between past and present: able, in other words, to *separate* the past from the present and, consequently, to understand the past *as* the past (see Hoffmann 2005). Although such commissions have represented often fragile and controversial experiments in the reconstruction of a shared political and cultural memory in the postcolonial space—i.e., the delineation of "figures of memory" within which the single individual memories and the collective memory can be anchored—they nonetheless constitute the most precious historical instance of a public exercise of "the work of memory and the work of mourning" (Ricoeur 2004, 505). They are able to suggest a reorganization (politically constructive and at the same time removed from the abstractly historicizing codes of a temporality that suppresses, absorbs, its past) of the three dimensions—at once historical, social, and individual—of the present, the past, and the future.

Part Two

Maps, Subjects, Translation

4
Translation and Transition

> Everything about human history is rooted in the earth, which has meant that we must think about habitation, but it has also meant that people have planned to have more territory and therefore must do something about its indigenous residents. At some very basic level, imperialism means thinking about, settling on, controlling land that you do not possess, that is distant, that is lived on and owned by others.
>
> —Edward W. Said, *Culture and Imperialism*

> "Colonialism" and "colonization" are only high points [*reliefs*], one traumatism over another, an increasing buildup of violence, the jealous rage of an essential *coloniality* . . .
>
> —Jacques Derrida, *Monolingualism of the Other, Or, the Prosthesis of Origin*

4.1. Writing Machines

In Orientalism (1978) Said repeatedly describes the Orient as a "textual universe," as the residue or precipitate—at once both material and doctrinal—of the West's irrepressible pulsion toward the *textualization* of alterity. Within this, according to the stereotype, the Western re-presentation (materialized in literary, ethnographic, philosophical, or economic–political texts and accounts) was infallibly set in opposition to an impenetrable and irredeemable Oriental *silence* (Said 1978, 52 and 94 *et seqq.*). This presumed "textualism" of Said's reflections (and of many of the exponents of postcolonial criticism) has over the years attracted the fiercest criticism of those who maintain that the prevalently textual, if not literary, interest of colonial discourse analysis came about and continues to operate at the expense of accurate historical–materialist research, everything being brought together in a radical obliteration of the intimately capitalistic trajectory of the imperial project (see, most recently, Parry 2004; but also Ahmad 1992; Lazarus 1999 and Dirlik 2000). Nevertheless, not only has Said incessantly asserted the historical–material density, or the "worldliness," of the textual fabrics analyzed (see Said 1983 and 2004), but he has also offered a definition of the concept of "Orientalism" (which came to coincide with the very term "colonialism") that complicates in the most fundamental way the framework outlined schematically above. Indeed, Said has often shed light and underlined the *systematic* nature of imperialism: its being, in the strict sense, a "machine" or a "system." It is precisely this "systemic" or "machinic" conception of Orientalism that has, after all, constituted the terrain on which we can read within it a more articulated and complex arrangement of *alterization*; it constitutes an "othering machine," to pick up on Spivak's formula (1999), which proceeds by means of the incessant production of boundaries and the differential incorporation of territories and populations within the framework of the imperial project.

Such a representation of colonialism as a "machine," however, has more than a few implications regarding a rethinking of the ambivalent concept of "textualization": above all where it brings to light how any "writing machine" (of the earth, of cultures, of meanings) is always, by implication a "translation machine." It has recently been underlined how *translation* is not only the political dynamic of postcolonialism (as a mapping of linguistic, cultural, geographical dislocations), but it is also a blind spot that postcolonial criticism proposes to illuminate (see Young 2003, 138 *et seqq.*). Indeed, if it is true that every translation process, far from taking place in a *vacuum*, unfolds in a *continuum* on which it inflicts cuts, schisms, breaks, departing from an originally dissymmetric relation (between texts, authors, or systems)—i.e., if it is true that this process, rather than referring to a relation of equality or equity, takes the form of a unidirectional process that always implies material and symbolic forms of *violence*—then the constitutive nexus that binds colonialism and translation appears ever more evident (Bassnett and Trivedi 1999, 2 *et seqq.*; see also Adamo 2007, 197 *et seqq.*). And this not only because of the fact that translation practices (of universal texts and cultures) have systematically supported the operations of conquest of native territories, but also—and much more deeply—because a colony itself is born as a translation, as the "copy of an original located elsewhere" (Bassnett and Trivedi 1999, 5). So it does not appear too fanciful to look at colonization as a process of *translational dematerialization* (Young 2003, 139): a process in which alterity (ethnic and cultural) is translated, "decodified," or again, "deterritorialized," according to linguistic and epistemological protocols that are extraneous to it. Alterity then finds itself "recodified" or "reterritorialized" in a position of radical subordination. Nevertheless, this model of "decodification" and "recodification," or of "deterritorialization" and "reterritorialization," cannot but recall a diagnostic scheme of the dynamics of capitalism that, deriving from Gilles Deleuze and Félix Guattari, has today been completely revised and relaunched from many quarters (Deleuze and Guattari 1983; Hardt and Negri 2000; Braidotti 2006). In *Anti-Oedipus* (1972)—a work, moreover, little read by postcolonialist authors—Deleuze and Guattari indeed set up a "dynamic model for the processes of colonization" (Young 1995, 170) that can function as an effective counterpart to the centrality often attributed preponderantly in the field of postcolonial criticism to the single dimension of "discursive construction" of alterity. And this insofar as in the first of the two volumes of *Capitalisme et schizophrénie* we find laid out an analysis of capitalistic devices that is immediately projected on a global surface, reconfiguring capitalism itself as a form of "cartography" or, even better, as an "epistemography" of the terrestrial globe in which material dynamics and imaginary dynamics are originally co-implicated:

> It is the function of the libido to invest the social field in unconscious forms, thereby hallucinating all history, reproducing in delirium entire civilizations, races, and continents, and intensely "feeling" the becoming of the world. There is no signifying chain without a Chinaman, an Arab, and a black who drop in to trouble the night of a white paranoiac. (Deleuze and Guattari 1983, 88)

Alongside a social theory of desire, a theory of the "group fantasy" that leads to "hallucinating history," "reanimating the races in delirium," "setting continents ablaze" (ibid., 105), Deleuze and Guattari elaborate a "geospatial" model of the dynamics of capitalism that includes within itself an analysis of colonialism. While it would be possible here to enter into the complex and controversial analysis developed in the *Anti-Oedipus*, it is best nevertheless to dwell on some of its fundamental theoretical coordinates and, in the first place, on the image delineated there of capitalism as, literally, a "writing machine," centered on the complementary functions of "decodifying" and "recodifying" social flows. Indeed, not only the decodifying of social flows in the abstract form of value (and the consequent "deterritorialization of the *socius*") constitute, for Deleuze and Guattari, the most intimate tendency of capitalism, but capitalism, in order to be able to guarantee its own survival, must at the same time invert and inhibit this tendency, bridling and reterritorializing that which has previously been deterritorialized:

> For capitalism constantly counteracts, constantly inhibits this inherent tendency while at the same time allowing it free rein; it continually seeks to avoid reaching its limit while simultaneously tending towards that limit. Capitalism institutes or restores all sorts of residual and artificial, imaginary, or symbolic territorialities, thereby attempting, as best it can, to recode, to rechannel persons who have been defined in terms of abstract quantities. Everything returns or recurs: States, nations, families. [. . .] there is the twofold movement of decoding or

deterritorializing flows on the one hand, and their violent and artificial reterritorialization on the other. The more the capitalist machine deterritorializes, decoding and axiomatizing flows in order to extract surplus value from them, the more its ancillary apparatuses, such as government bureaucracies and the forces of law and order, do their utmost to reterritorialize, absorbing in the process a larger and larger share of surplus value. (Deleuze and Guattari 1983, 34)

If this *twofold movement*, as we shall see, is co-extensive to capitalism as "axiomatic immanent" of decodified flows (flows of money, of work, of products), it is necessary, in this context, to pay attention to two preliminary aspects. In the first place, the centrality that in this model is granted to the physical–geographical question of *space*: by virtue of which it is possible to affirm that "The earth is the primitive, savage unity of desire and production" (ibid., p. 140). This centrality, indeed, not only refers to the original act of violent expropriation and of territorial conquest on which the colonial enterprise stands, recalling how colonialism has above all involved the *physical* appropriation of the earth, the destruction of native territories and their reinscription in agreement with the needs of the apparatus of the occupying power (see Young 1995, 172). But it also marks a well-defined thesis on the nature and the modes of functioning of modern power. Since if it is true that in the works written *entre-les-deux* by the couple Deleuze-Guattari there is a passage from a statal or "molar" paradigm of power as expropriation, partition, division, and appropriation (in the direction of a power Foucauldianly spread throughout the entire social body), the *Anti-Oedipus* functions to highlight how one does not substitute the other, but rather reinforces it: how power as division/appropriation of the earth remains the mute and obscure basis of widespread micropowers. It was, after all, a Marxist geographer such as David Harvey who underlined how it is precisely in the tension between the "territorial logic of power" and the "capitalistic logic of power" that there sits the matrix of that *compulsive spatialization* that is part and parcel with the historical advance of capitalism (Harvey 2003, 184). Earlier, in his celebrated *The Condition of Postmodernity*, Harvey had written (quoting Deleuze and Guatteri):

> If space is indeed to be thought of as a system of "containers" of social power [. . .] then it follows that the accumulation of capital is perpetually deconstructing that social power by re-shaping its geographical bases. Put the other way round, any struggle to reconstitute power relations is a struggle to reorganize their spatial bases. It is in this light that we can better understand "why capitalism is continually reterritorializing with one hand what it was deterritorializing with the other." (Harvey 1990, 237–38)

In other words: capitalistic accumulation proceeds through a continuous movement of appropriation and reconfiguration of spaces previously external and extraneous to the logic of capital, manifesting the perpetual need to have something "outside of itself" to be able to guarantee its own stabilization. Or again, manifesting the necessity of constantly producing its own "other," which acts in this way as an ambivalent *constitutive exterior* (on the concept of "constitutive exterior" see, for example, Laclau 1995; Butler, Laclau and Žižek 2000). It is from this point of view that Harvey can maintain that today's globalization of capital operates as a new phase in accumulation "by dispossession or expropriation," recalling with this the profile of what Marx defined "original" or "primitive accumulation" (*ursprüngliche Akkumulation*). This is a phase in the process of accumulation which, placed by Marx at the dawning of capitalism and characterized by the use of massive doses of violence in expropriations and enclosures of the common weal, is reappearing today on the worldwide level (see Harvey 2003; but on the contemporary nature of the Marxian concept of "original" or "primitive accumulation" see, among others, Bensaïd 2007 and Mezzadra 2008). On the other hand, it is always from this perspective that it is necessary and useful to look at the transformations intervening in the logic and the geography of global spatiality: a spatiality that, as Ahiwa Ong is effective in maintaining, is far from taking a smooth, friction-free form. This spatiality, on the contrary, rather proves itself to be crossed and interrupted systematically by "latitudes," by *striated* and *lateral spaces* inside which different regimes of disciplining and regulating work are combined. Within these, above all, there prevails a *logic of the exception* on the basis of which there takes shape the incessant production of "leftovers" or—to borrow Zygmunt Bauman's words—of "wasted lives" (Bauman 2004), which do not belong (except under the banner of a prison-like and pre-modern discipline of work) to the circuits of production and accumulation (Ong 2006). To return to Harvey, it is along this line of reflection that he formulated the need to elaborate a renewed form of "historical–geographical materialism" (Harvey 1996 and 2006): i.e., an analysis able to record the shattering effect that the introduction of spatial and geographical considerations produces in the context of predominant social theory, traditionally interested in exclusively *temporal* processes of transformation—or, perhaps it would be better to say, of "transition"—founded on the axiom of an abstractly homogeneous historical–geographical background.

Nevertheless, before approaching the crucial question of *transition* from a postcolonial perspective, it is useful to examine a second aspect inferable from Deleuze and Guattari's book, because this can lead us to the problematic of the *textualization* of alterity and to the configuration of capitalism—and orientalism—as veritable "writing machines," or "translation machines." The paradigm of "decodifying" and "recodifying" social flows is in fact clearly a semiotic–textual paradigm, the dynamic of which is rendered operative by what could be defined as a function of *translation*. This does not mean to dwell, here, on the well-known analogy between linguistics and economy (see, among others, Saussure 1959, 79: "Here as in political economy we are confronted with the notion of value; both sciences are concerned with a system for equating things of different orders—labor and wages in one and a signified and signifier in the other.") Nor is it a question of simply highlighting contemporary post-Fordist forms of "semio-capital," by virtue of which it is possible to maintain that today language and communication, "are structurally and contemporaneously present throughout both the sphere of the production and distribution of goods and services and the sphere of finance" (Marazzi 2008, 14). Rather it is necessary to verify which idea—or ideology—of translation has taken form and has found its own historical–material correspondent in imperialist capitalism as "translation machine." But to do this it is useful to return to what Marx himself wrote, confuting any direct "comparison" between money and language, in a passage from the *Grundrisse*: "To compare money with language is not less erroneous. Language does not transform ideas, so that the peculiarity of ideas is dissolved and their social character runs alongside them as a separate entity [. . .] Ideas do not exist separately from language. Ideas which have first to be translated out of their mother tongue into a foreign language in order to circulate, in order to become exchangeable, offer a somewhat better analogy; but the analogy then lies not in language, but in the foreignness of language." (Marx 1973, 162–63.) In other words, in order for there to be trade and circulation, it is necessary to constitute a "general equivalent" (that "arcane of the form of goods," analyzed in *Capital*, which operates as an implacable equalizer) with regard to which goods take on the attitude of "ideas" to *translate* into a *foreign language*: the language, abstract and no less real, of "value." It is precisely this idea of a "universal translatability," founded on the ideology of a *generalized equivalence*, that after all would be at the basis—according to an eminent exponent of French "translatology" like Antoine Berman—of a profoundly ethnocentric figure of translation, hinged on a Platonic primacy of *sense* that would unleash the typically European impulse toward the omnivorous interception of the other. The history of Western translation thus had a hidden face, a dark side, that took shape—from pagan Romanity onward as the "culture of ransacking," passing through the evangelizing impulse of Christianity up to the catastrophes of colonialism and imperialism—in a "conquering and unscrupulous translationism," dominated by a fundamental pulsion toward the *annexation of the foreign* (Berman 1999). Significantly, this trope of a "universal translatability" is found again in the centrality assumed today—beginning with Jakobson's reflections on translation (see Jakobson 1971, 262: "Equivalence in difference is the cardinal problem of language and the pivotal concern of linguistics")—by the linguistic figure of "equivalence." According to this figure, translation true and proper is provided only wherever it is possible to establish fixed criteria of conversion between terms offered as equivalents.

It is precisely this value of "equivalence"—a controversial theoretical proposition in the midst of all the contemporary theories on translation—that thus constitutes the crossing point between a certain ideology and a certain practice of translation (which, in Berman's wake, it is legitimate to call "ethnocentric translation") and the dynamics of capitalism and colonialism. We have seen, indeed, how the function that renders the mechanics of "deterritorialization" and "reterritorialization" of capital operative resides in the purely abstract form of *value*, which per se is a bare value of *equivalence*: equivalence of goods and meanings, of territories and cultures—equivalence, ultimately, of bodies. If then, on the basis of reading Robert Young, it is possible to see in imperialist capitalism and *a fortiori* in colonialism, "translation machines," this comes about because they materialize an ideology that reduces sociocultural reality to a system of Jakobsonian equivalences, thus configuring themselves not only as "translation machines," but also—and more correctly—as destroyer machines of social and cultural signification (see Young 1995, 173). Over the course of the years in a series of celebrated essays, Spivak re-questioned Marx's work. Her point of departure was the proposition of the *textuality of the chains of value* and she gained leverage from the Marxian idea of the abstract form of value as *inhaltslos und einfach*: as an empty medium on which the specific modes of production and codification exercise themselves, be they economic, social, or cultural (Spivak 1993b; 1996a and 2000b). Without being able here to enter into Spivak's complex arguments, what must be emphasized is not only the identification of the abstraction and the codification (and the correlated normative and privative language of "abstract" equality) as vehicles, to use the lexis of Jacques Derrida, of a "phantomalization" or of a "spectralization" of social bonds (see Derrida 1994, 196–99: "For the thing as well as for the worker in his relation to time, socialization or the becoming-social passes by way of this spectralization. [. . .] what *Capital* is analyzing here is not only the phantomalization of the commodity-form but the phantomalization of the social bond, its spectralization in return"). But also the nexus that the critique of an "abstracting" translation of the differences operated by capital through the value-form as bare equivalence dwells on the question (historical and social) of *transition*. Indeed, in her well-known essay, "Deconstructing Historiography," Spivak acknowledges that a considerable part of postcolonial criticism—and specifically the work carried out by the theoreticians of Subaltern Studies—aimed in the first instance to delineate the profile of a "theory of transition" within capitalism. Or rather, it was a *plural* declension of such a transition, thus related to differential histories of domination and of exploitation rather than within the framework of the "grand narrative" of the means of production. Here Spivak holds firmly to a "textual" perspective (in the wider sense we have sought to illustrate), defining the transition as "a functional change in a sign system" (Spivak 1988, 4). More specifically:

> A theory of change as the site of the displacement of function between sign-systems [. . .] is a theory of reading in the strongest possible general sense. The site of displacement of the function of signs is the name of reading as active transaction between past and future. This transactional reading as (the possibility of) action, even at its most dynamic, is perhaps what Antonio Gramsci meant by 'elaboration,' *e-laborare*, working out. If seen in this way, the work of the Subaltern Studies group repeatedly makes it possible for us to grasp that the concept-metaphor of the 'social text' is not the reduction of real life to the page of a book. (ibid., 4–5)

Nevertheless, it is probably in the work of Chakrabarty that a similar nexus between "translation" (or "e-laboration") and "transition" comes to light in a manner that is simultaneously both more cogent and more crystalline.

4.2. Global Capital and "Historical Difference"

The irreducibly ambivalent role played by the category of translation in the logical and historical–material constitution of global capital is to be found thematized effectively by Chakrabarty within the framework of an examination of the paradoxes linked to the narrative (Weberian and Marxian) of the "transition" to capitalism, or, in other words, the narrative of "modernization." Indeed, what is at stake here for the Indian critic does not reside purely in contesting the "historicist" and "secular" propositions that lead us to place the history of political modernity in non-Western societies under the heading of "incompleteness" and "lacuna": "the 'failure' of a history to keep an appointment with its destiny" (Chakrabarty 2000, 31). Thus further crucial questions are touched on, such as the *logic* of universalism and the *anthropological* foundation on the basis of which this last is periodically legitimized and invoked. But let us proceed here in an orderly fashion. Chakrabarty's argument in *Provincializing Europe* occupies the ground of an analysis of the constitutionally ambivalent structure of the relation between capital and differences: wherein if on the one hand capital tends to reduce and obliterate differences in the exclusive code of abstraction, on the other hand not only does it contain and negotiate them, but it requires them as a condition of its very own functioning. Nevertheless, here it is not so much a matter of reading into capitalism a mere *logic of integrated excess*, which sees the unrestrainable proliferation of cultural, ethnic, sexual differences (recodified as "tastes" and "preferences" in the multicultural *grand bazaar*) provide the ephemeral material on which the *basso ostinato* of a system capable of reproducing itself through a constant self-revolution is played (see, for example, Žižek 2002). The stress here falls, rather, on the *historical* character of difference: in other words, on its being a sign of a plurality of geocultural trajectories and of forms of "belonging" which, precipitating through all "staged" schemes, constitute "the site of an ongoing battle" (Chakrabarty 2000, 65). Chakrabarty's position is, in effect, clear and explicit: "The problem of capitalist modernity cannot any longer be seen simply as a sociological problem of historical transition (as in the famous 'transition debates' in European history) but as a problem of translation as well" (ibid., 17). It is in this context that a vigorous comparison with the Marxian category of "abstract labor," or of "abstractly human labor" is located: and this because of the fact that "abstract labor" is both the precipitate, or the crystallization, of the Enlightenment figure of the abstract individual—of that "system of equality and freedom" that constitutes the correlate of the system of circulation of capital (Marx 1973, 239–50)—and that *tertium* mediator which, *translating* the differences in a code or in a common measure, has the value of *normative equivalence*. In other words, "abstract labor" functions as an implacable *medium* of equalization, allowing the capitalistic language of "value" to "extract from peoples and histories that were all different a homogenous and common unit" (Chakrabarty 2000, 50). In the attempt to deconstruct the Marxian narrative of "transition," the Indian historian's preliminary move is to intend "abstract labor" as a *practical, performative* category: "To organize life under the sign of capital is to act as if labor could indeed be abstracted from all the social issues in which it is always embedded and which make any particular labor—even the labor of abstracting—concrete" (ibid., 54). "Abstract human labor" thus reveals itself in its nature as *disciplinary abstraction*, since the *as if* of life organized under the sign of capitalism does no less than hark back to those "despotic" processes of *disciplining*—that "subtle, calculated technology of subjection," which, according to Foucault, accompanied the movement "of accumulation of capital" (Foucault 1977a, 221)—the role of which is to reveal precisely how abstraction (the reduction of subjects to a "norm," or their "translation" into the abstractly human) is a constitutive element of the mode of functioning of capital.

And nevertheless, Chakrabarty underlines, the category of "abstract labor" operates at one and the same time as *description* and *critique* of capital: to the extent that "the labor that is abstracted in the capitalist's search for a common measure of human activity is *living*" (Chakrabarty 2000, 60). In Marx's words, capital searches for "*non-objectified labour*, labour which is still objectifying itself, *labour as subjectivity*," which is "inseparable from the worker's own bodily existence" (Marx 1973, 272 and 46); as Paolo Virno writes in an important analysis of the Marxian category of "labour-power," here it is the same "living body, pillaged of every one of its qualities except pure vitality" that becomes "the *substratum* of productive capacity, the tangible *sign* of potential, the objective *semblance* of non-objectified labour." (Virno 2015, 161–72) In this way, the very process through which capital produces "abstract labor" as a *norm* carries within itself the seed of "resistance" as "Other of the despotism inherent in capital's logic," since "life [. . .] is the excess that capital, for all its disciplinary procedures, always needs but can never quite control or domesticate. [. . .] Life, in Marx's analysis of capital, is similarly a 'standing fight' against the process of abstraction that is constitutive of the category 'labor,'" (Chakrabarty 2000, 59 and 60–61.) It is nevertheless precisely against this rooting of "resistance" to the logic of capitalistic abstraction in *life*, or rather in the "non-chronological" dimension of an abstract "capacity to work" (see in this sense Virno 2015, 183–89) that the Indian historian directs his criticism. And this to the extent to which, from this perspective, the "historical difference" remains absorbed and suspended. It is in this context that in *Provincializing Europe* we see introduced the crucial distinction between "History 1"—which is to say "homogenous and empty time" *imposed retrospectively* by the logic of capital—and differing "Histories 2," which represent the same number of "histories of belonging" that qualify signal modalities of *inhabiting* capitalistic modernity (see also Chakrabarty 2002). The *universe of the pasts* met by capital along its trajectory is indeed greater than the sum of the elements that it sets as its own conditions and requirements, acknowledging another series of "relationships that do not lend themselves to the reproduction of the logic of capital," and modalities of being-in-the-world that are irreducible to that of "human bearer of labor power" (Chakrabarty

2000, 64 and 66). Gaining leverage on the ambiguity of Marx's prose, the historicist *not yet* is here reinterpreted in a deconstructivist manner: as that which, marking an intrinsic deferment to the logic of capital, indicates at the same time that the absorption of "Histories 2" within the homogenizing narrative of "History 1" will never be complete or absolute. With these coordinates the ambivalent nexus between "translation" and "transition" is clarified:

> Translation makes possible the emergence of the universal language of the social sciences. But it must also, by the same token, enable a project of approaching social-science categories from both sides of the process of translation, in order to make room for two kinds of histories. One consists of *analytical* histories that, through the abstracting categories of capital, eventually tend to make all places exchangeable with one another. History 1 is just that, analytical history. But the idea of History 2 beckons us to more *affective* narratives of human belonging where life forms, although porous to one another, do not seem exchangeable through a third term of equivalence such as abstract labor. Translation/transition to capitalism in the mode of History 1 involves the play of three terms, the third term expressing the measure of equivalence that makes generalized exchange possible. But to explore such translation/transition on the register of History 2 is to think about translation as a transaction between two categories without any third category intervening. (Chakrabarty 2000, 71)

Thus a model of translation governed by the logic of equivalence is opposed by another modality of translation: an intimately "anti-sociological" translation which—far from seeking dialectical leverage on a middle term that has a value of equivalence ("life," or "abstractly human labor")—presents itself as a transaction and exchange "without any third category intervening," and which presupposes and produces "the partly opaque relationship we call 'difference'" (ibid., 17). The differing "Histories 2," or the *subaltern pasts*, indeed do not constitute an Other dialectic with respect to the history of capital, being rather at the same time supplement and suture or, to use a musical term dear to Said, the *counterpoint*: constantly interrupting, and modifying, the totalizing pulsions of "History 1." But from here there also flow considerable consequences with regard to a rethinking and a redefinition of the very lexis of *universalism*. No global capital, Chakrabarty writes, can ever embody or represent a "universal" logic of capital, since every *historically* available form of capital "is a provisional compromise made up of History 1 modified by somebody's History 2s" (ibid., 70). The universal is thus configured as a "place holder" (in the not very faithful but certainly fortunate Italian translation, an "empty box"), "its place always usurped by a historical particular seeking to present itself as the universal" (ibid.):

> Capital brings into every history some of the universal themes of the European Enlightenment, but on inspection the universal turns out to be an empty place holder whose unstable outlines become barely visible only when a proxy, a particular, usurps its position in a gesture of pretension and domination. And that, it seems to me, is the restless and inescapable politics of historical difference to which global capital consigns us. (ibid.)

The characterization of the universal as an "empty place," as a synonym of the constitutive incompleteness, of the necessary negativity at the heart of the political—necessary negativity to the extent to which it prevents the collapse of the political into a totalizing and totalitarian ethno-communitarian substance—is, after all, a *topos* characteristic of that part of radical thought which in recent decades has sought to conceive of democracy beginning from a revisitation, fully aware of the poststructuralist revolution, of the notions of hegemony and ideology: i.e., with a blend of Gramscism and poststructuralism capable of making use of the riches of both approaches as its point of departure (see Laclau and Mouffe 1985;

Laclau 1995; Butler, Laclau and Žižek 2000). And nevertheless, against the linguistic–structural or Lacanian variants of this *topos*, here there is a declension of the thought of the "incompleteness of the universal" that begins with the two registers (much more convincing) of *temporality* and of *translation*. On the one hand, indeed, looking at the universal in a *temporal* modality involves taking the "not yet" as an essential moment of its own articulation; or again, it implies looking at that which remains "unrealized" of the universal (the voice of those who are not included by it, who lack the titles necessary for occupying a place of enunciation, and who nonetheless demand inclusion) as that which constitutes it in an essential manner, haunting it as the *spectral double* of the particular to which it is opposed (see Butler 2000, 24; and 2004a, 233). On the other hand, a conception centered on the insuperability of *translation* (between cultures, languages, universes of value) cannot but recall a hermeneutic perspective which, in contrast with the abstract, formal and procedural universalisms, insists on the assumption of a constitutive equivocalness of the universal. As Balibar has written, to suggest ". . . that the universal is essentially *equivocal* does not mean saying that *universals* divide up universality, like a lost origin or a horizon of future sense, but rather that each one *is* and *is not* the universal. In other terms, it is only aporetically and above all it is only by proximity, by interference, by problematic 'identification' with the others, with that which is not all its own self. Thus the 'universal'—if there is one and it is 'one'—would be the tie, or the passage from one figure to another. But this passage itself has no figure, no unity, no stability. It is only slips, conflicts, ambiguities or lacerations." (Balibar 1997, 450; but see also Balibar 2006a.) It is in this sense that the universal can be articulated only within a "politics of translation." And, as Balibar again underlines, the very idea of translation simply recalls dialectical categories such as *conflict* and *reciprocity*, weaving itself in an essential way with the question of *boundaries* and, even more profoundly, with the problem of the current decomposition and recomposition of boundaries that render unstable any topology founded on a simple separation between "interior" and "exterior," or "inclusion" and "exclusion" (see Balibar 2006b, 6 *et seqq.*). After all, here it is necessary to pay attention to the very notion of *boundary*, in its relationship with the category of translation: to the extent to which the concept of boundary—symbolically interrelated with the problematic of translation within its etymon, *trans-latio*—recalls, to pick up on Walter Benjamin, that "nucleus of the untranslatable" of languages that makes of translation itself an *infinite and never concluded task*, suspended in the opacity of languages and vocabularies:

> It is plausible that no translation, however good it may be, can have any significance as regards the original. Yet, by virtue of its translatability the original is closely connected with the translation; in fact, this connection is all the closer since it is no longer of importance to the original. We may call this connection a natural one, or, more specifically, a vital connection. (Benjamin 1968, 71)

And this is a connection, we read further on, that regards survival, an "afterlife" for the work, in which: "Translation is so far removed from being the sterile equation of two dead languages that of all literary forms it is the one charged with the special mission of watching over the maturing process of the original language and the birth pangs of its own" (ibid., 73).[1] From this point of view, what significance does a "politics of translation" acquire? And what consequences flow from it regarding a redefinition of the lexis and the semantics of the universal? If, as Benjamin writes, translation "is only a somewhat provisional way of coming to terms with the foreignness of languages," wherein—and here Benjamin quotes Rudolf Pannwitz—the translator allows "his language to be powerfully affected by the foreign tongue" (ibid., 75 and 81), this happens because—far from dealing with relations of exact equivalence—it superimposes the foreign on the foreign, configuring itself as a *historical–dynamic* model of transformation in which what is translated reemerges, as *different,* from its other. It is along this line of reflection that the universal, conceived according to the paradigm of translation, takes the figure of a permanent reconstruction, of an "invention" that forces and nourishes itself with incommensurability and foreignness, or—in line with what Chakrabarty maintains—with a transaction (and with a transition) "without any third category intervening." But from here a hermeneutic perspective opens up, touching directly on the *symbolic* dimension of a "politics of translation."

5
Politics of Translation

> Indeed the very meaning of "home" changes with experience of decolonization, of radicalization. At times, home is nowhere. At times, one knows only extreme estrangement and alienation. Then home is no longer just one place. It is locations.
>
> —bell hooks, *Yearning*

> I have always said that the Caribbean Sea is different from the Mediterranean because it is an open sea, a sea that diffracts, while the Mediterranean is a sea that concentrates. If the civilizations and the great monotheistic religions were born around the Mediterranean Basin, this is due to the capacity of this sea for orienting, albeit through dramas, wars or conflicts, the thought of man toward the One and unity.
>
> —Édouard Glissant, *Introduction à une poétique du divers*

5.1. Cultural Identity and Ambivalence

Boundaries, barriers, frontier zones constitute the symbolic and material correlative with which the linguistic and corporeal experience of colonized subjects is woven: for example, the *new mestiza* of which Gloria Anzaldúa has written (1987), or the migrant as *translated being* par excellence in Salman Rushdie's formula (1991). With them and through them translation takes form in its historically *ambivalent* figure, on the one hand as crystalline form of expropriation and linguistic and cognitive violence (to the extent to which the location-as-subject of the migrant or of the colonized subject is in itself an epistemically fractured location) and, on the other, a movable palimpsest of inscriptions and reinscriptions capable of producing shifts in processes of cultural signification. Along these coordinates runs the track of postcolonial reflection on translation that has sought and seeks to hold together a revision of the concept (nebulous and crucial at one and the same time) of "culture," with a renewed thematization of the question of identity, in relation to the linguistic and symbolic dynamics that are simultaneously sites of formation and negotiation. In a climate marked by the emergence of new "struggles for recognition" (Taylor 1992; Honneth 1992; Fraser and Honneth 2003; Benhabib 2002) and fierce "politics of identity" (I. M. Young 1990), issues relating to cultural identity indeed suddenly found themselves projected into the limelight of the international scene. And nevertheless, there wherein the vocabulary of multiculturalism "culture" is for the most part conceived of as founding and insuperable dimension of *authenticity*, in line with a vision steeped in Romantic–Herderian presuppositions regarding unity and uniqueness of the *Volk*, of the "community" and the language, in the context of postcolonial criticism the category of "culture" is declined according to an "adjectival" paradigm (Appadurai 1996, 12 *et seqq.*); or, better still, an *enunciative* paradigm (Bhabha 1994, 85), as a dynamic process of struggle and of construction of meanings. A process which—far from putting down its own roots in static and consolidated ground, in an ontologized *Weltanschauung*—concerns, to paraphrase James Clifford, both its roots and its roads: which is to say the unstable articulation of transnational memory and connections that renders each culture a "travelling culture," formed and modeled by meetings with alterity (Clifford 1997).[1] From this point of view, which sees the proliferation of a "new world order of mobility, of rootless histories" (ibid., 1), it is necessary to look at the proliferation of figurations that gain leverage on de-centralizing categories such as "diaspora," "flows," "transculturations," "contact zones," or "strategies" *para entrar y salir de la modernidad*, to "enter into and exit from modernity" as Néstor García Canclini writes with regard to the "hybrid cultures" of Tijuana that daily contest every vision of modernization as a strictly unidirectional process (Canclini 1990; see also Hannerz 1996). Here, however, it is useful to dwell on the very concept of "transculturation," brought back into vogue and developed by the United States anthropologist Mary Louise Pratt along the lines of an analysis of cultural phenomena as phenomena that pertain principally to "contact zones" among cultures (Pratt 1992). The neologism "transculturation" was coined in the 1940s by the Cuban anthropologist Fernando Ortiz, openly contrasting with "diffusionist" conceptions that looked upon cultural contact in terms of linear processes of "acculturation" of the "receiving" culture, which is to say as unidirectional phenomena intimately disposed toward a logic of conquest and domination. As Bronislaw Malinowski writes in his preface to Ortiz's evocative *Cuban Counterpoint: Tobacco and Sugar*:

> Every change of culture, or, as I shall say from now on, every transculturation, is a process in which something is always given in return for what one receives, a system of give and take. It is a process in which both parts of the equation are modified, a process from which a new reality emerges, transformed and complex, a reality that is not a mechanical agglomeration of traits, nor even a mosaic, but a new phenomenon, original and independent. To describe this process the word *trans-culturation*, stemming from Latin roots, provides us with a term that does not contain the implication of one certain culture toward which the other must tend, but an exchange between two cultures, both of them active, both contributing their share, and both co-operating to bring about a new reality of civilization. (Ortiz 1995, lviii–lix)

In an important book aimed at the more wide-ranging objective of "decolonizing knowledge" and dedicated to a strict and innovative examination of eighteenth-century European travel writing on the non-European world, Mary Louise Pratt magisterially developed this intuition, coming to define "transculturation" as a "phenomenon of the contact zone" (Pratt 1992, 6) and described this contact zone as that "space" in which peoples geographically and historically separated from one another establish, with high levels of improvisation, new and unprecedented relations; relations, nevertheless, almost always marked by conditions of coercion, of domination and of radical inequality. In this sense the term "contact zone"—borrowed from its current use in linguistics where "contact languages" are those "improvised" languages (such as pidgins or creoles) through which speakers of different native languages come to communicate among themselves—refers to the phenomenon of the "space and time where subjects previously separated by geography and history are co-present" (Pratt 1992, 7); subjects whose interactions develop "often within radically asymmetrical relations of power" (ibid.).

It is in this regard, in the analysis of transcultural relations, that the demands of rhetoric and power make their entrance, signifying a *dynamic* and *conflictual* vision of cultures that cannot but have crucial repercussions on modalities of conceptualizing the notion of identity.[2] From this point of view, we must look above all to the work of the theoretician and lynchpin of Cultural Studies, Stuart Hall. Indeed, it is especially because of the fact that in his theoretical pattern it is possible to discern not only a non-essentialistic conception of (cultural) identities (rather than a *strategic* and *positional* conception), but also a precise declension of the problematic of enunciation. Here the concept of "identity," indeed, fades and acquires consistency in the notion of *identification*, moving to indicate—to borrow from Hall's lexis—the point of "suture" or of "articulation" (and thus not already of subsumption) between subjects and discursive practices or, more specifically, between subjects and mechanisms of power (see Hall 2006a and 2006b). Identity thus becomes primarily a *position of enunciation*, where—according to the lesson of Structuralism—the subject that enounces and the subject of the enunciation are never found in the same position; and therefore in a place where the subject always appears shifted, always dislocated with regard to a predefined space and time:

> The past continues to speak us. But it no longer addresses us as a simple, factual "past," since our relation to it, like the child's relation to the mother, is always-already "after the break." It is always constructed through memory, fantasy, narrative and myth. Cultural identities are the points of identification or suture, which are made, within the discourses of history and culture. Not an essence but a *positioning*. Hence, there is always a politics of identity, a politics of position, which has no absolute guarantee in an unproblematic, transcendental "law of origin." (Hall 1990, 226.)

From this point of view, cultural identities—"far from being eternally fixed in some essentialised past" (ibid., 225)—offer themselves as movable sites of identification through which cultural codes and meanings are constantly renegotiated, according to the continuous "play" of history, of culture and of power; or better, they offer themselves as the ever-mutable "names we give to the different ways we are positioned by, and position ourselves within, the narratives of the past," (ibid.), according to the praxis (individual and collective) that Eric Hobsbawm vividly named as the "invention of tradition" (see Hobsbawm and Ranger 1983). But, in the wake of what has been described, it is useful now to turn to a similar "enunciative" and "positional" paradigm with regard to the notions (identitary and essentialist) of cultural "authenticity" and "purity."

5.2. Language and Minorities

The "politics of position"—which Stuart Hall, as we have seen, declares as being separate from any "law of origin"—unfolds in a privileged manner with regard to the linguistic *medium*, conceived of not so much as a neutral or normative background of communication, as rather a vehicle of a veritable "poietics" of identity. It is along a similar trajectory of reflection that the category of "hybridization" acquires relevance. This is a category to which we would like to dedicate some attention here, with regard to its relations with a strictly performative conception of language and enunciation.[3] Far from having a merely eulogistic or neutralizing value, the notion of "hybridity" or "hybridization" indeed refers, in the wake of Mikhail Bakhtin's work, to a "dialogizing" of language that is anything but a harmonic resolution of the forces that dwell in it, constituting rather the wellspring, the field, and the nourishment of social contradictions and "pluridiscursivity." The "socio-linguistic" hybrid, wrote Bakhtin, is not purely "double-voiced" and "double-accented": "but it is also double-languaged; for in it there are not only (and not even so much) two individual consciousnesses, two voices, two accents, as there are two socio-linguistic consciousnesses, two epochs, that, true, are not here unconsciously mixed (as in an organic hybrid), but that come together and consciously fight it out on the territory of the utterance." (Bakhtin 1981, 360; on this topic see the classic Todorov 1981.) This struggle on the territory of the utterance is what configures the process of the "hybridization" of languages and cultures as a preeminently *political* and *disputational* dynamic, within which (as occurs in the carnival and in heteroglossia) one voice unmasks the other, delineating its boundaries and revealing its silences and its points of fracture. With these coordinates, Homi Bhabha recovers the category of "hybridization," linking it with a double thread to the paradoxes of translation and making of it at the same time an instrument for casting light on the constitutively *ambivalent* structure of every discourse of authority and, in particular, of the discourse of colonial authority (Bhabha 1994, 145–73). Bhabha defines "hybridity" as "a problematic of colonial representation and individuation that reverses the effects of the colonialist disavowal, so that other 'denied' knowledges enter upon the dominant discourse and estrange the basis of its authority." (ibid., 162.) "Hybridity," in other words, constitutes the moment in which the discourse of authority, opening itself up to processes of appropriation and translation on the part of the "indigenous" cultures, disassociates itself from the regime of uniqueness, loses its hold on a univocal meaning, and displays its own original ambivalence. Indeed, the disarticulation of the voice of authority is produced, according to Bhabha, not so much through spectacular overturnings, as through tactical shifts, "little differences," modalities of appropriation and of resistance, of "mimicry"[4] or of "sly civility" that gain leverage on the centrifugal forces present in every act of enunciation: forces by virtue of which the appropriation (or the translation) of the dominant discourse in the codes of the subaltern language gives rise to effects of transformative repetition and of dislocation of authority:

> Mimicry marks those moments of civil disobedience within the discipline of civility: signs of spectacular resistance. Then the words of the master become the site of hybridity—the warlike, subaltern sign of the native—then we may not only read between the lines, but even seek to change the often coercive reality that they so lucidly contain. (Bhabha 1994, 172)

In this perspective, translation, producing effects of repetition and dislocation, becomes the hub of a practice of "resistance"—or of subversion of hegemony—through which the "natives" appropriate the text of authority, subverting it from within and using it to expose its own fragility: as in the case of the native Hindu vegetarians who, faced with the Book of the Christian God, demanded an "Indianized" version, a Hindi Bible that did not come from "the flesh-eating mouths of the English." (ibid., 166.) The translation (or hybridization) between the colonial culture and "native" cultures thus proceeds as a shift in the value of authority from symbol to sign: a shift by virtue of which the untranslatable (or incommensurable) between the cultures emerges in the language as that which breaks the register of the symbolic and the semantic, sundering at the same time the identities of the subject of authority and the subaltern subject. It is in this sense that Bhabha can maintain that "the effect of colonial power is seen to be the production of hybridization rather the noisy command of colonialist authority or the silent repression of native traditions" (ibid. 160); and it is in this sense, in the wake of Albert Memmi (2004), that all simple distinctions or linear antitheses between colonizer and colonized are abandoned, beginning with an understanding of language as the privileged site of struggle and countervailing power.

This diagnosis of the conflictual economy of colonial power—centered on an iterative and transformative function of translation/mimicry of the dominant codes—is founded, on closer inspection, on a precise declension of the category of "minority": a declension that insists on the nexus between *language* and *minority*, or between power and dominant languages. Although there are no specific references in Homi Bhabha's works, this reflection on language and translation has considerable resonance with the framework, polarized in the pair "major" and "minor," used by Deleuze and Guattari to fathom the "minor literatures" of Kafka or of Beckett as mediums through which social and cultural conflict are articulated (see Deleuze and Guattari 1986). Indeed, the "minor languages" have nothing to do with the nostalgic recovery of some original tongue, rather they constitute a tensional polarity within a continuous process of linguistic variation that explodes any "unity" of language. The "systematic" principle—that which organizes languages into a "system"—is nothing less, for Deleuze and Guattari, than the extraction of a set of "constants" from linguistic variables, or the determination of constant relations between these variables.

> But the scientific model taking language as an object of study is one with the political model by which language is homogenized, centralized, standardized, becoming a language of power, a major or dominant language. [. . .] The unity of language is fundamentally political. There is no mother tongue, only a power takeover by a dominant language that at times advances along a broad front, and at times swoops down on diverse centers simultaneously. (Deleuze and Guattari 1987, 111–12)

And nevertheless, once again from *A Thousand Plateaus*, there open up between the "power" of the constants and the "force" of the variants, fault lines and zones of passage. These are "transitional spaces" through which it comes to light how the "major" and the "minor" are not already states, but purely "usages" and "functions" of language (ibid., 115 *et seqq.*). It goes without saying that similar "transitional spaces"—within which we see the "minor language" soften up and strain the "constants" of the dominant language to the point of deforming them—constitute the site of renegotiation of the identities of the colonizer and the colonized par excellence. The Caribbean poet Derek Walcott—"I who am poisoned with the blood of both, / Where shall I turn, divided to the vein?" (Walcott 1986, 18)—plays with alliteration in an exemplary fashion, or with a metonymic axis that digs and empties the semantic force of names, to make the language of the colonizer and the colonized quake and shake:

> Anguilla, Adina,
> Antigua, Cannelles,
> Andreuille, all the *l*'s,
> Voyelles, of the liquid Antilles,
> The names tremble like needles
> Of anchored frigates
>
> (ibid., 44)

The relationship between language and survival, negotiated in a space of tension between the "major" and the "minor" that carries within itself the sign of the guilt "For all whom race and exile have defeated, / For my own uncle in America, / That living there I could never look up" (ibid., 65), which unfolds like a crossing through of languages that makes use of the techniques of the *détour*, of diversion or, in the words of Édouard Glissant, of "hidden creolization" (see Glissant 1996). The phenomenon of linguistic blending and hybridization, indeed, takes place prevalently in what are called "interlanguages": in deracinated and emigrant languages, in the *sabirs* or lingua francas, in Creole, in the "fusion langages" and in the various slangs that, from a sociological point of view, are often identified with the "criminal classes."[5] These "interlanguages" constitute *non-normed zones* of language, which are also spaces of struggle that can be measured in terms of power and hegemony. And it is for this reason that Bhabha finds in postcolonial poets and writers such as Walcott, Rushdie, and Naipaul the emergence of "another history of the sign" against the history of imperial nominalism (Bhabha 1995, 52): "another history" that opens up to "hybridization" as a process of negotiation of cultural identities that proceeds *beyond any binary logic*:

> If [. . .] the act of cultural translation (both as representation and as reproduction) denies the essentialism of a prior given original or originary culture, then we see that all forms of culture are continually in a process of hybridity. But for me the importance of hybridity is not to be able to trace two original moments from which the third emerges, rather hybridity to me is the "third space" which enables other positions to emerge. (Bhabha 1990, 211)

The "third space," or the *in-between* space, of translation is thus an interstitial space by nature: a passage from which crossing points of symbolic resistance open up together with spaces of linguistic subversion that penetrate the language of the dominators, subjecting their canon and discursive regime to stress. Caribbean Creolization—which finds its own voice in poets such as Derek Walcott and Edward Kamau Brathwaite (see Brathwaite 1984)—is, in this context, the clearest example of a "two-way" movement of translation that also constitutes an active site of counter-power.[6] The Creole language, indeed, is a "translated" language, born out of the contact between completely heterogeneous elements: a language suspended in a state of turbulence that derives from systems constantly having to face up to one another. As Glissant writes in tracing the coordinates of an "archipelagic thinking," opposed to the dominant "continental" thought, not only is "every language in origin a creole language"—which is to say a language "translated" through alterity—but creolization itself (and translation) constitute a constant transition, an "art of flight from one language to another without the first being erased and the second giving up the idea of putting itself forward":

> Translation is flight, therefore a renunciation. What seems above all necessary to glean in the act of translating is the beauty of this renunciation [. . .] I would say that this renunciation is, in the world-totality, the part of the self that is abandoned, in any poetics, to the other. I would say that this renunciation, when it is supported by sufficient reasons and inventions, when it emerges in the language of sharing I have spoken of, it is the thought itself of touching, the archipelagic thinking through which we recompose the landscapes of the world, a thinking which, against all system-thoughts, teaches us the uncertain, that which is threatened, but also the poetic intuition towards which we now sail. (Glissant 1996, 18 and 36)

5.3. Logic, Rhetoric, Silence

Although, as we have seen, postcolonial translation has risen over the years to become a general epitome of the fluctuating and decentered condition of subjects that are permanently "in the diaspora" (apparently relegated to the margins and the periphery of the "empire"), it has wound its way, and still does wind its way, above all as a long and still-unfinished battle around the formation and deconstruction of the Eurocentric literary and epistemological "canon." Or, to borrow the formula of the Kenyan writer and essayist Ngũgĩ wa Thiong'o, postcolonial translation battles in the effort to "move the center" of the world (Ngũgĩ wa Thiong'o 1993). Indeed, characteristically postcolonial here is an attention for the role and the "hegemonic" definition of literature, itself taken within an "imperialist narrativization" of history. From this point of view, literary translation and reinscription take the form of a sophisticated practice of *rewriting*—or, in the effective and untranslatable English formula, a *writing back*—the Western "canon," which aims to unmask its silences and discursive discontinuities: as comes about in the case of the rewriting of Charlotte Brontë's classic *Jane Eyre* in Jean Rhys's *Wide Sargasso Sea*, or in the case of *Foe* by John Maxwell Coetzee, in which the South African writer reinscribes the postcolonial allegory in one of the founding myths of the Western imaginary, Daniel Defoe's *Robinson Crusoe*.[7] Following the tracks of literary reinscription it clearly comes to light how the objective of postcolonial "rewriting" is not so much (or not only) the insertion of a voice of opposition, or the insertion of a different version of the history narrated, but rather—and much more radically—an entrance into the dominant discourse that violates its parameters and boundaries, gaining leverage on the same qualities of rhetoric of the language and on the effects of concealment and silencing that it produces. As asserted by Gayatri Spivak, the introduction of literary rhetoricity acts as a "tropological" deconstruction, laying bare the strategic silences and exclusions of the "imperialist continuity," to the point that "rhetoric may be disrupting logic in the matter of the production of an agent, and indicating the founding violence of the silence at work within rhetoric." (Spivak 1993a, 181)

And nevertheless, it is precisely the postcolonial literary reinscription that demonstrates—against any conciliatory and peace-making ideology of the revision or the linear widening of the dominant canon—how rewriting can never be full or complete. Rather we find that rewriting clashes with a "Law" inscribed in the same politicized weave of language. In *In the Heart of the Country* (1977), Coetzee narrates in exemplary fashion the story of a woman who, in the desolation of the lands of South Africa, fights "against becoming one of the forgotten ones of history," and he masterfully brings into focus the nexus that binds the colonial experience to a violent functioning of *language* as *political and symbolic law*:

The lips are tired, I explain to him, they want to rest, they are tired of all the articulating they have had to do since they were babies, since it was revealed to them that there was a law, that they could no longer simply part themselves to make way for the long *aaa* which has, if truth be told, always been enough for them, enough of an expression of whatever this is that needs to be expressed, or clench themselves over the long satisfying silence into which I shall still, I promise, one day retire. I am exhausted by obedience to this law, I try to say, whose mark lies on me in the spaces between the words, the spaces or the pauses, and in the articulations that set up the war of sounds, the *b* against the *d*, the *m* against the *n*, and so forth [. . .] The law has gripped my throat, I say and do not say, it invades my larynx, its one hand on my tongue, its other hand on my lips. (Coetzee 1982, 84)

But it is above all in *Foe*, as mentioned above, that Coetzee poses the problem of the reinscription of silence within the Western literary canon, focusing his narrative on the instances of gender and race. The protagonist, indeed, is no longer Crusoe—normative paradigm of imperial bourgeois individualism—but a woman, Susan Barton, who, after her shipwreck on Crusoe's island and the death of the latter at sea, returns to London together with Friday and attempts to transpose her memories of the island into written form. And the center of those memories turns out to be Friday himself, he whose tongue has been cut out and is therefore closed in the lonely circle of mute dance and echolalia:

The story of Friday's tongue is a story unable to be told, or unable to be told by me. That is to say, many stories can be told of Friday's tongue, but the true story is buried within Friday, who is mute. The true story will not be heard till by art we have found a means of giving voice to Friday. (Coetzee 1986, 118)

The story of the "native," of Friday, is thus the enigma or the hole in the narration from which springs the generative desire of Susan Barton, a desire translated into a writing with a particular inversion of genders and parental positions, which lead her to state: "By such means do I still endeavour to be father to my story. [. . .] I was intended not to be the mother of my story, but to beget it" (ibid., 123 and 126). Spivak, in her reading of Coetzee's novel, casts light on the aporias of textuality, the difficulty with which feminism and anticolonialism are able to occupy "a continuous (narrative) space" within a narrative that attempts to reinscribe the history of capitalism and of the colony (Spivak 1999, 185). Nevertheless, here we must pay attention above all to the exasperation and the craving with which the woman attempts to *restore voice and word* to the "native," to construct him as the "subject of a story." Indeed, at the ending an anonymous narrator tells of a second shipwreck, at once real and imaginary, in which Susan Barton herself and Friday lie dead:

> But this is not a place of words. Each syllable, as it comes out, is caught and filled with water and diffused. This is a place where bodies are their own signs. It is the home of Friday.
> He turns and turns till he lies at full length his face to my face. The skin is tight across his bones, his lips are drawn back. I pass a fingernail across his teeth, trying to find a way in.
> His mouth opens. From inside him comes a slow stream, without breath, without interruption. It flows up through his body and out upon me; it passes through the cabin, through the wreck; washing the cliffs and shores of the island, it runs northward and southward to the ends of the earth. Soft and cold, dark and unending, it beats against my eyelids, against the skin of my face. (Coetzee 1986, 157)

Coetzee's text, a postcolonial allegory of the *untranslatable*, thus stages the desire and the impossibility—the impossible desire—of invading the margin ("This is a place where bodies are their own signs.") and the impropriety of the dominant impulse to give voice to the "native" and to translate from a position of monolinguistic superiority. Friday, Spivak writes observantly, with his inability to pronounce the letter *H*, is also perhaps "a reminder of the alterity of history" (Spivak 1999, 189).[8]

It is precisely along these theoretical and conceptual coordinates that Spivak's celebrated essay, "Can the Subaltern Speak?" (now in Spivak 1999), unfolds with its dialogue form and its polemic with the work of the Subaltern Studies group. In particular, Spivak here articulates a critique of the "speculative" logic of the founder of the group, Ranajit Guha, according to whom the project behind Subaltern Studies was to obey Benjamin's injunction to "recover the subtracted past," to "expropriate the expropriators," to give voice to the "excluded from world history," tracing the *awareness* of the subaltern in its dialectic development, back to its pure state. Spivak finds it easy to object that the task of the historian cannot be (according to the protocols of the most classic metaphysics) "to recover a presence" or a lost "origin," but must consist rather of the disarticulation of the semiotic chain—of the Nietzschean *Zeichenkette*—within which the subject, be it subaltern or elite, is constituted. Spivak nevertheless goes beyond this: she questions at their roots the methodological suppositions of the historiographical and theoretical–political Subaltern Studies project itself. Gaining leverage on the case of the abolition by the English colonial power of the Indian rite of *sati* (the burning of the widow on her husband's pyre), she indeed reaches the conclusion that the subaltern—here to be precise the *female* subaltern—"cannot speak." According to what was written, then rectified, then rewritten by Spivak, the fact that the subaltern woman "cannot speak," obviously does not mean an incapacity of the subaltern woman to have her say, nor that she leaves no trace in the historical–social fabric, but the (theoretically much more relevant) awareness that—within the protocols of the dominant language, be it historical, ethnographic, or *sic et simpliciter* political—she has not been assigned any *position of enunciation*; or, in other terms, she is constituted as the "*nonsuit of the broadcasting of an alternative discourse*" (Carravetta 2009, 322).

Beyond the polemics that have accompanied this statement regarding a presumed "silence" of the subaltern—which is to say, regarding the radical irrecoverability of their experience—it is nevertheless necessary here to dwell on the meaning that the term "speak" acquires in this context. Faithful to a Gramscian framework, Spivak as we have seen adheres to a conception of the "fabric" or of the "social text" for which the notion—only apparently textual—of *e-laboration* (i.e., an unfolding of hegemonic relations) fulfills a role that is to say the least crucial. In this view the "speaking" of the subaltern indicates nothing less than a possible *transaction* between the subject who enounces and the subject who reads/listens: or, in other words, a transaction between the "submerged" of history and those who intend to recover their voices. Stating that the subaltern cannot "speak" thus marks above all a breach that has taken place in relations between those who are "past"—those who lived on the margins or the periphery of History, or who still live there—and the present: a breach the principle attribute of which is a well-defined figure of modern theory and politics. This explains the attack made against the representative and/or representational paradigm of political theory, aimed signally at two figures, Deleuze and Foucault, unanimously considered spokespersons of a "non-representational" theory, and of a "non-representative" politics. Dissecting their well-known dialogue on "Intellectuals and Power" (1972), Spivak notes fault lines in it too, or lines of exclusion that contribute to preserving "the subject of the West, or the West as Subject" (Spivak 1999, 261). Where Deleuze stated: "We ridiculed representation and said it was finished, but we failed to draw the consequences of this 'theoretical' conversion—to appreciate the theoretical fact that only those directly concerned can speak in a practical way on their own behalf." Foucault then rejoined: "When people begin to speak and act on their own behalf [. . .] they do not oppose a new representativity to the false representativity of power" (Deleuze and Foucault 1977, 209 and 211). And Spivak denounces in both of them a dangerous obliteration of the problematic of ideology, which is part and parcel with "an unquestioned valorization of the oppressed as subject" and an intellectual form of "ventriloquism of the speaking subaltern" (Spivak 1999, 255; but for the contemporary value of a reflection that examines the mechanisms of ideology, see in general Žižek, ed. 1994). But what precisely is going on in this accusation aimed at authors who have, after all, within the panorama of postcolonial theory, provided research tools and indispensable categorical forms for a critique of the Eurocentric Subject and its apparatuses of power and conquest? Evidently not only the identification of a theoretical and political ingenuousness in the mechanism for liquidating "representation"—in its double status as *Vertretung* and of *Darstellung*, of political representation and of conceptual representation (for a framing of this see Accarino 1999)—by virtue of which it would be enough to declare obsolete or "outmoded" the mechanism of delegation/representation to be able to restore voice and word to the oppressed or, to borrow from Fanon, to "the wretched of the Earth." Also at work here, and much more profoundly, is the denouncement of the preemptive attribution of an undivided and monolithic subjectivity to the oppressed—thus a subterranean alter ego of the western "subject of knowledge"—which corresponds, writes Spivak, to an incapacity to "imagine the kind of Power and Desire that would inhabit the unnamed subject of the Other of Europe" (Spivak 1999, 265).

It is in this sense that, to pick up on a category from the work of Jean-François Lyotard, the status of "subalternity" might be defined as a case of *dissension*, or of *différend*: wherein, as Lyotard writes, "what I would like to call *différend*" is "the case where the plaintiff is divested of the means to argue and becomes for that reason a victim. [. . .] A case of differend between two parties takes place when the 'regulation' of the conflict that opposes them is done in the idiom of one of the parties while the wrong suffered by the other is not signified in that idiom" (Lyotard 1988, 9). Or again:

> The differend is the unstable state and instant of language wherein something which must be able to be put into phrases cannot yet be. This state includes silence,

> which is a negative phrase, but it also calls upon phrases which are in principle possible. [. . .] What is at stake in a literature, in a philosophy, in a politics perhaps, is to bear witness to differends by finding idioms for them. (ibid., 13)

The "silence" of the subaltern is then nothing else than the "diaspora" of political language that impedes some agents from signifying their conditions or the wrongs they have undergone, unless it be in the idiom and the language of the other. In the moment in which individuals or groups (be they "natives," women, or migrants) are divested of the possibility of "saying" and signifying their experience in an idiom that is not the dominant one, then we have a mechanism of "subalternization": which is today a mechanism of *deprivation of subjectivity* (or of *de-subjectivization*) that impedes any political "power of speech." It is in this sense that Gayatri Spivak's insistence on the "silence" of the subaltern becomes an allegory of *untranslatability*: wherein, however, the question is not one of "essential" untranslatability (metaphysical and originary), but rather regards the "history of the untranslatability" of subaltern discourse in the canons of the imperialistic discourse (see, for an analogous reading, Chow 1993, 35–38).

But to return to the coordinates with which this section opened—centered on the politically and linguistically constitutive relation between logic, rhetoric, and silence—and to fathom the implications with regard to a rethinking of the discourse surrounding subjectivity, it is useful to give attention to another definition that Spivak traces for the "subaltern" subject. In "Deconstructing Historiography," attacking the emphasis placed by Ranajit Guha on "coherence" and on "logic" that will "inevitably objectify the subaltern and be caught in the game of knowledge as power," Spivak indeed asserts that it "is necessarily the absolute limit of the place where history is narrativized into logic" (Spivak 1988, 16). On closer inspection, at stake here is not only the albeit crucial question of the limits of historiography, centered on the awareness that adding a subaltern "supplement" to elite history cannot mean adding, in mere arithmetic terms, fragments of submerged histories to the *continuum* of official history. Also at stake is a particular and specific declension of the problem of *subjectivization*. It is not by chance that over the years, Spivak—spurred by the question, *Who decolonizes? And how?*—has turned increasingly frequently to postcolonial writers to articulate with an *affirmative* formula the question of subaltern subjectivity, since it is precisely in a certain postcolonial, women's writing that the parties of power and subject appear inverted, opening a passage to the thought of a possible "politics of subjectivization." Consider, as a particularly eloquent example, "Draupadi" by the well-known Bengali writer and activist, Mahasweta Devi. This story recounts the brutal violence perpetrated on the flesh of tribal women and men in colonial India and it concludes with Draupadi, hunted down and imprisoned, exposing herself naked and proud to authority. Her body has been violated, her belly and breasts are bleeding, and with this gesture she silences power, returning it to its condition of naked violence:

> Draupadi stands before him, naked. Thigh and pubic hair matted with dry blood. Two breasts, two wounds.
>
> [. . .]
>
> Where are her clothes?
>
> Won't put them on, *sir*. Tearing them.
>
> Draupadi's black body comes even closer. Draupadi shakes with an indomitable laughter that Senanayak simply cannot understand. [. . .] What's the use of clothes? You can strip me, but how can you clothe me again? Are you a man?
>
> [. . .] There isn't a man here that I should be ashamed. I will not let you put my cloth on me. What more can you do? Come on, *counter* me—come on, *counter* me—?

> Draupadi pushes Senanayak with her two mangled breasts, and for the first time Senanayak is afraid to stand before an unarmed *target*, terribly afraid. (Devi 1981, 402)

In reading Devi's story one has the impression of an overturning of planes, of a sort of *mise-en-abyme* of the narrative, insofar as in the last lines of the story, the reader comes to the awareness that the only authentic subject therein is the tribal woman, and that the "silence"—to overturn Spivak's formula—is the most intimate essence, not of the subaltern, but of power. The subaltern subjectivization thus takes the form of a "self-translation": a sort of "pedagogy of the oppressed" (or empowering from below) that cannot but have repercussions on the codification of notions such as "subjectivity" and "citizenship."

6

Political Subjects

Today, how do I, as water douser, craft words out of so many tones of voice still suspended in the silences of yesterday's seraglio? Words of the veiled body, language that in turn has taken the veil for so long a time.

Here, then, is a listening in, by means of which I try to grasp the traces of some ruptures that have reached their term. Where all that I could come close to were such voices as are groping with the challenge of beginning solitudes.

[. . .] Don't claim to "speak for" or, worse, "speak on," barely speaking next to, and if possible *very close to* . . .

—Assia Djebar, *Women of Algiers in Their Apartment*

6.1. Geography of Dominion, Cartographies of Subalternity

The epistemic violation carried out in the theatre of colonization and decolonization has been effectively summarized by Gayatri Spivak in the category of "enabling violation" (Spivak 1999, 217; 2003b, 169). For Spivak, if access to the European Enlightenment (with its correlated ideals of freedom and equality) through colonization constituted a paradoxical form of "enablement," this "enablement" at the same time coincided with and was overwritten by a fierce form of *violation*, material and epistemic, of the colonized subjects. The most urgent political claims in the decolonized space (constitutionality, citizenship, democracy) are in fact, Spivak reminds us, tacitly recognized as coded *within* the legacy of imperialism: concept-metaphors for which no historically adequate referent may be advanced from postcolonial space (see Spivak 1993c, 158). It is in the context of a "dystopian" representation of colonization of this kind that the "tactical" use of the category (of Gramscian heritage) of "subalternity" acquires relevance: here, in the wake of Michel de Certeau, the "tactic" is distinguished from the "strategy" (model of political, economic, scientific rationality) insofar as it cannot count on a place of its "own" (a spatial or institutional localization), as point of departure for the calculation of relations of strength with respect to a distinct exteriority—to the extent that "the place of a tactic belongs to the other" (de Certeau 1984, xix). The term "subaltern"—re-elaborated, as we have seen, in the attempt to "rewrite" the struggle for independence of colonial India beyond and against the nationalistic historiographical, Marxist, and elitist models—sought above all to bring into the light that "autonomous space" of action and resistance to which it was possible to ascribe a "politics of the people" independent of the politics and the codes of signification of the elites (see Guha 1988b). In particular, in the early works of the Subaltern Studies Collective of historians, polemic attention was aimed in the first place at that spontaneist prejudice which tended to inscribe peasant revolts and insurrections within a sort of "natural history" made up of "outbreaks," "uprisings," "propagations," thus depriving them of autonomous forms of politicality; a prejudice that was instead opposed by a search for the "essential" structure of the peasant consciousness and the dynamic and unpredictable modes assumed by its political agency. In this way, the Gramscian concept of "subaltern" (made to coincide with the notion of "people") allowed an avoidance of the bottlenecks of economic reductionism and the teleological framework still imputable to a strictly Marxist theoretical instrumentation, maintaining at the same time the focus of the analysis on the phenomena of exploitation and domination (see Young 2001, 354–55; and above all Sarkar 2000, where there is a fierce critique of the "postmodern" drift of the work of Subaltern Studies; but in general see Chaturvedi, ed. 2000).

We have seen how much of the polemic within the work of the group was worked out around the speculative logic, almost Hegelian, that had governed the attempt, in particular on Guha's part, to map the "essential development" of the subaltern "consciousness," in contrast with a vision of the insurrection "as *external* to the peasant's consciousness and Cause is made to stand in as a phantom surrogate for Reason, the logic of that consciousness." (Guha 1988c, 47). Nevertheless, despite the theoretical impasses deriving from the attempt to "recover" the subjectivity of the subaltern, it is precisely in the definition of this last that we find some of the most precious contributions offered by postcolonial studies with regard to a rethinking of the paradigm (Western and Eurocentric) of the universal and constituent subject, whose correlate is a clearly determined conception of power and politics. The definitions of subaltern "consciousness" that periodically have been offered invariably reveal themselves to be *differential, subtractive, negative*. If initially Guha identified the "subaltern classes" with "*the demographic difference between the total Indian population and all those whom we have described as the 'elite'*" (Guha 1988b, 44), subsequently he wrote more explicitly about the subaltern: "His identity amounted to the sum of his subalternity. In other words, he learnt to recognize himself not by the properties and attributes of his own social being but by a diminution, if not negation, of those of his superiors" (Guha 1997, 18). As Spivak writes, "consciousness here is not consciousness-in-general, but a historicized political species thereof, subaltern consciousness" (Spivak 1988, 11), never fully recoverable and always dislocated with regard to the received meanings: a "negative" consciousness that can perhaps provide "the model for a general theory of consciousness" (ibid.). Conceived of in this way, as a "presence without essence" (O'Hanlon 2000, 89) or as a "position without identity" (Spivak 2008, 239), the category of "subalternity" becomes also a theoretical instrument capable of unmasking the current-day political dynamics of "global" inequality and exclusion, entering into dialogue and in resonance with some attempts—carried out in a purely philosophical context—at rethinking the foundations, and, above all, the *topology* of democracy (see Fornari 2005).

It is nevertheless thanks above all to the deconstructive operations of Chakrabarty and Spivak that the category of "subaltern" has progressively acquired its own depth in the theoretical field, crossing the boundaries of the revision of the historiographical canons of the Indian subcontinent and moving to intersect with an analysis of the logics that govern late "global" capitalism. The point of departure here should be the perspective offered by Chakrabarty, because he brings to light forcefully how the field of tension informed by the term "subaltern" is purely *philosophical* as well as—if not primarily—historical and anthropological. In *Provincializing Europe* the Indian historian indeed details, clearly and explicitly, that the subaltern "is not the empirical peasant or tribal in any straightforward sense that a populist program of history writing may want to imagine. The figure of the subaltern is necessarily mediated by problems of representation" (Chakrabarty 2000, 94). Thus we have a first indication: as happens for Spivak, here too the notion of "subalternity" (purged of any socio–anthropological connotation) refers to the problem of "re-presentation," in its double status as *Vertretung* and of *Darstellung*, of "delegation" and of "staging." It refers, i.e., to that paradox of the "*lieu*-tenancy"—of using words *in the name of others*—which every historiography and every politics has always been obliged to face up to. But there is more: escaping imprisonment in any sociological definition, the term "subaltern" seems here not to designate anything more than a "place," a "position," the content of which cannot but be dictated by some "anthropological difference" held from occasion to occasion, and thus contingently, to be discriminatory (see Balibar 1997, 13). On the other hand, after having characterized the Subaltern Studies project as an attempt to trace a "genealogy of the 'masses' as political actors" (Chakrabarty 2004, 233) and having denounced the potentially "populistic" outcomes, Chakrabarty subjects the very notion of "subaltern" to an important twist. Indeed, in a radically anti-essentialist move, the Indian historian defines the "subaltern" as "a collective subject with no proper name, a subject who can be named only through a series of displacements of the original European term 'the proletariat' " (ibid., 243), implying with this the impossibility of *naming* in an essentialistic manner a presumed revolutionary subject. In an analogous anti-essentialist gesture, Spivak, on her part, defines the "subaltern" as that "space" that has been "cut off from the lines of mobility" (Spivak 1996b, 288). In other words: the condition of "subalternity," far from being able to define itself in a substantive form, has within itself a purely *adjectival* value, indicating those segments and those fractions of a society and of the world that, excluded from social mobility, are at the same time excluded from all structures of "responsibility"—subjects that *are* not, but *become* subaltern, no longer being able to answer *to* or *for* anything.

What are the theoretical cues to be drawn from this brief summary of two of the many definitions outlined, within Subaltern Studies, of the term "subaltern"? And which indications can be derived from this regarding a rethinking of today's lexis and semantics of democracy? In the first place, thanks to Chakrabarty's warning on the dangers connected to populist historiographical programs that identify in strict socioanthropological terms the "subaltern," it is possible to recognize in this last an "empty signifier," a floating signifier open to metonymic shift. Put in other terms: if there is no definition of the category of "subalternity" that does pass through the bottleneck of "representation," this signals above all the impossibility of *naming* in an essentialistic way the oppressed or the excluded from the "pyramid of civilization"—except, indeed, through a structurally open series of keywords, such as woman, native, migrant, and so forth. To this radically anti-essentialistic argument, Spivak nevertheless adds a further component, centered on the awareness of a *foreclosed* signifier, a "subaltern of the subaltern" (the native woman, for example). The question regarding this figure is not to re-present—in the two senses already mentioned of "delegation" and "staging"—the presumed "consciousness" or "experience," but rather to call into play a well-defined theory of politics and of democracy. A theory which, far from resolving itself in the caricature of anarchic and fluctuating differences, sees politics construct itself on a series of *radical exclusions* (or, to use Judith Butler's words, of "mechanisms of abjection": see Butler 1993), which return however to haunt politics with their own absence.

This according to the psychoanalytic lesson by which whatever is foreclosed in the Symbolic, and is not directly representable, is destined nevertheless to signify itself in the Real as interruption and subversion of the processes of signification. Not by chance does the Chinese theoretician Rey Chow define the "native" as *symptom*, like the Lacanian *sinthome*, as that which gives ontological consistency to the subject (in this case to the European colonial and neocolonial Subject-Master), marking the site of its constitutive absence (Chow 1994, 127 *et seqq.*). And it is in this sense that in postcolonial thought there is not so much a desire to expose a mere effect of exclusion of the other, as rather a denouncement of the *power of inclusion* that is in itself more fiercely exclusive than any ostentatious gesture or marginalization carried out by means of historical practices and materials of restriction.

This figure of an *excluding inclusion*, or of an *including exclusion*, or, better still, of a *differential and selective inclusion* of subjects in the normed space of sovereignty and power, is to be found nowadays illustrated figuratively and materially by the radical processes of transformation affecting the traditional modern concepts of rights and citizenship, beginning with the new and in certain respects unprecedented regime of today's transnational migrations. Not by chance Spivak was able to state recently that "the new subaltern is produced by the logic of a global capital that forms classes only instrumentally" (Spivak 2000a, 330), pointing with this to the much vaster and limitless question of the seismic upheavals that today distress the social geography of the global world, and stymie every attempt at recomposing lines along the interpretative schemes and trajectories inherited from tradition. Indeed, it is precisely the "case" of the transnational migrations that constitutes the special terrain on which it is possible to verify the constitution in the strict *postcolonial* sense of the fault lines and the new fractures that furrow contemporary societies (see Mezzadra 2008). And this insofar as the incessant flows of people—which intersect along trajectories that are anything but "smooth" and linear with the massive flows of capital—between and along the *boundaries* of the North and the South of the world, lead to a "disaggregation" of the juridical space that is part and parcel with a *decomposition* of the unitary figure of the modern citizen and citizenship (see, for example, Balibar 2004, 2003 and 2005; Benhabib 2004 and 2006; Ong 2006; Mezzadra, ed. 2004 and 2008; Rigo 2007). In particular, the proliferation of a plurality of categories of subjective juridical status (citizens, semi-citizens, "legal" migrants, to the extreme logical limit of the "illegal clandestine") reproposes a juridical fragmentation previously typical of the colonial and imperial nations, ritualizing the colonial distinction between citizen and subject, or—as Balibar writes—indicating "the persistence of the empty place of the *subject [sujet]*, forming the shadow cast by the citizen in the space of sovereignty" (Balibar 2004, 40). In this sense it becomes possible to denounce a "recolonization of social relations" (ibid., 41) or, more specifically, a "recolonization" of migrations (see Balibar 2003; Sassen 1996), corresponding, yes, to a radical disarticulation of the elements (rights, entitlements, territoriality, nation) that traditionally composed the modern institution of citizenship (see Ong 2006, 14 *et seqq.*), but also a specular and concomitant decomposition of the very figure of the *foreigner*, which was flanked by some *foreigners less than foreign* (barely different, "neighbors," therefore similar to us and assimilable) and by *foreigners more than foreign* (radically "other" from us, therefore non-homogeneous and unassimilable) (see Balibar 2006b, 4); but on the *structurally* ambivalent character, and therefore irreducibly "unsayable," of the figure of the "foreigner" in the framework of the Western political tradition (see also Honig 2001). If, as Balibar again writes, "the figure of the 'citizen' (with its statutory conditions of birth and place, its different subcategories, spheres of activity, processes of formation) is exactly a way of categorizing individuals," and if on the other hand, "such a process is possible only if other figures of the 'subject' are violently or peacefully removed, coercively, or voluntarily destroyed" (Balibar 2009, 192), then one would find oneself today in a condition that gives rise in a disturbing way to "traditional patterns of exclusion which contradict the formal equality associated with the constitutions of the democratic nation-states. For example, the categories of 'citizens' and 'subjects' in colonial nations manifests this contradiction, where the border was also a concentric *double border* (between the metropolis and the subjected territories, between the Empire and the rest of the world)" (Balibar 2006b, 4).

Thus it appears evident in this perspective the extent to which it is possible to define the entire spectrum of contemporary society (and first of all the society of an "enlarged" Europe) as a set of "*postcolonial situations*" (Balibar 2004, 24), or as though structurally marked by a profound "colonial fracture" (Blanchard, Bancel and Lemaire, eds. 2005) rendered extremely sensitive by the contemporary movements of populations. Also evident is the question of to what extent a strictly *topological* (non-essentialistic and non-substantive) definition of the "subaltern" such as that which here has been tentatively offered, can provide some theoretical instruments for rethinking the delineation and the constitution of contemporary democracies. And it is in this sense that, having reached this threshold, it appears useful to turn to a consideration of some theoretical–political elements that are "constructive" in the wider sense, inferable from the grand unfinished canvas of subaltern and postcolonial studies. The aim here is yes to fathom the relationship of tension, but also that of reciprocal co-implication between symbolic order, politics and logics of the universal.

6.2. The Political Word

The implications of "subaltern studies" for a theory of "resistance" and of "liberation" are enclosed within the same category—wide-ranging and in itself metonymic—of "insurrection." And within this term it is necessary to include those radically democratic moments in which subalternity is brought to *points of crisis* (see Spivak 1988, 4; 1996b, 289 *et seqq.*)—i.e., those moments in which the attempt to move the "excluded" within the perimeter of citizenship coincides with a concomitant renegotiation and redefinition of the same codes of abstract universalism. From this point of view, it is perhaps Étienne Balibar who clarifies most cogently what is at stake here, when he writes:

> The authentic discourse of the dominated [of the "subaltern"], "prior" to any hegemonic use, cannot be isolated as such. It appears mainly as a "forgotten" origin, or is testified to not so much by actual words as by practical resistance, the irreducible "being there" of the dominated . . . The actual relationship between dominant and dominated in the field of ideology must remain ambivalent in history, but there is undoubtedly a meaning of universality which is intrinsically linked with the notion of *insurrection*, in the broad sense ("insurgents" are those who collectively rebel against domination in the name of freedom and equality). This meaning I call *ideal universality*—not only because it supports all the idealistic philosophies which view the course of history as a general process of emancipation, a realization of the idea of man (or the human essence, or the classless society, etc.), but because it introduces the notion of the *unconditional* into the realm of politics. (Balibar 2002, 164–65)

And nevertheless, where Balibar in this passage—despite the identification of the universal with an "unconditional," an "empty box," or to use Chakrabarty's words, a *place-holder*, ready to welcome the unforeseen movements of subjectification of social subjects—seems to place in suspension or under *epoché* the possibility of an "authentic discourse of the dominated," it is precisely around the principle of an autonomous and radical *power of speech* of the oppressed and the "subaltern" that there unwinds the most theoretically fertile line of postcolonial studies. As we shall see, in the work of critics such as Chakrabarty, Bhabha, and Spivak, as in that of philosophers such as Balibar himself and Jacques Rancière, it is possible to trace a political thought on "subjectification" which, distancing itself from the modern paradigm of the universal and constituent subject as well as from a postmodern dissolution, insists on the insurmountable nexus between *constitution of the subject* and *articulation of the universal*: or, in other terms, on the originary and indissoluble unity of ontology and politics. After all, throughout the history of philosophy attention has been brought to bear many times on the unity, in the "subject," of the *subjectum* (individual substance or material substrate of accidents) and of the *subjectus* (juridical term that refers to the subjection by and submission to a sovereign power), as a play on words—materially active but disavowed throughout the entire spectrum of philosophical enquiry—that directs the gaze toward an enigma: "why is it that the very *name* which allows modern philosophy to think and designate the *originary freedom* of the human being—the name of 'subject'—is precisely the name which *historically* meant suppression of freedom, or at least an intrinsic limitation of freedom, i.e., *subjection*?" (Balibar 1994, 8; but on the unity, in the "subject," of subjectification and subjection, see also Butler 1997). This "enigma" corresponds to a conception of *freedom* not as already a possession or a status, but as a result of a process of "liberation," of an emancipation, of a *becoming-free* that departs from subjection and maintains with subjection an insurmountable relation. It is along these lines that in a part of postcolonial thought the thematization of the condition of "subalternity"—as a radical deprivation of subjectivity and of speech—is tied to a thinking of the universal that is inextricably linked to a thematization of the processes of subaltern "subjectification" (or "power of speech"). But let us dwell, initially, on the very term "power of speech," borrowing words written by a philosopher such as Michel de Certeau in the climate of 1968:

> Speech that had become a "symbolic place" designates the space created through the distance that separates the represented from their representations, the members of a society and the modalities of their association. It is at once everything and nothing because it announces an unpacking in the density of exchange and a void, a

disagreement, exactly where the mechanisms ought to be built upon what they claim to express. It escapes outside of structures, but in order to indicate what is *lacking* in them, namely, solidarity and the participation of those who are subjected to them. (de Certeau 1997, 9–10)

"Unpacking," "disagreement," "void" are after all some of the keywords around which important and stimulating attempts at rethinking the political logics operating at the basis of contemporary democracies have recently been articulated. This beginning with the experience of the unforeseen and unpredictable *capture of speech* on the part of subjects otherwise thought of as radically lacking in *logos*: subjects who had been deprived in an authoritarian manner of the onto-political status of having "power of speech." Jacques Rancière in particular has redefined politics with as his point of departure the proposition of the irreducible existence of a "part-of-those-who-have-no-part," which reveals how counting the "parts" in the social order—the distribution of the roles and the functions of the social body—is always a false computation, affected by a radical *contingency*: "There is politics when there is a part of those who have no part, a part or party of the poor. [. . .] Politics exists when the natural order of domination is interrupted by the institution of a part of those who have no part. [. . .] Beyond this set-up there is no politics. There is only the order of domination or the disorder of revolt." Or again: "Politics exists because those who have no right to be counted as speaking beings make themselves of some account, setting up a community by the fact of placing in common a wrong that is nothing more than this very confrontation, the contradiction of two worlds in a single world: the world where they are and the world where they are not, the world where there is something 'between' them and those who do not acknowledge them as speaking beings who count and the world where there is nothing" (Rancière 1999, 11–12 and 27). More than this: politics only begins with the "gap created by the empty freedom of the people" (ibid., 19), expression that cannot but recall what the Indian theoretician Partha Chatterjee has called, in the wake of work carried out on the "autonomous space" of the politics of the "subaltern," "popular politics" (Chatterjee 2004, 3): intending with this an experience of politics, and of democracy, irreducible to the standards and the canons of the modern liberal democracy and bearer therefore of instances and forms of heterogeneous "politicality" irreducible to those codified in European and Western experience (but on the more general theme of "the democracies of others," see also Sen 2003). If, as Spivak writes, "the place of the subject of rights is empty because [. . .] it must be written in the normative and privative language of abstract equality" (Spivak 2000b, 11), here this privative language is opposed by a dynamic of *creating rights*, founded on the venture of an active transformation of the processes of exclusion into processes of inclusion within citizenship. Indeed, several times Spivak's position, for example, has been uncharitably accused of failing to contemplate any space for an autonomous *agency* of the subaltern. But on closer inspection, the theoretical framework adopted here aims instead at inverting the mark of that *epistemic discontinuity* that characterizes the "class segregation" separating the elites from the subaltern (a transversal segregation with regard to the now untenable distinction between the First and the "other" worlds), in the direction of a sort of "pedagogy of the oppressed" that follows a logic of empowering from below (see Spivak 2003b); in line with an analogous logic—tracing in a "democratization of knowledge" founded on the "revolt of subaltern knowledge," the possibility of escaping the imperialistic "monocultures of the mind"—are the analyses of the eco-feminist Vandana Shiva in Shiva 1993, 59–64).

Politics, then, becomes a matter of *subjects*, or again, of *modes of subjectification*. To quote again from Rancière:

> By subjectification I mean the production through a series of actions of a body and a capacity for enunciation not previously identifiable within a given field of experience, whose identification is thus part of the reconfiguration of the field of experience. Descarte's *ego sum, ego existo* is the prototype of such indissoluble subjects of a series

of operations implying the production of a new field of experience. Any political subjectification holds to this formula. It is a *nos sumus, nos existimus*, which means the subject it causes to exist has neither more nor less than the consistency of such a set of operations and such a field of experience. [. . .] A political subjectification is the product of these multiple fracture lines by which individuals and networks of individuals subjectify the gap between their condition as animals endowed with a voice and the violent encounter with the equality of the logos. (Rancière 1999, 35–37)

If politics is an occurrence or a singularity through which subjects reactivate "the contingency of the equality, neither arithmetical nor geometric, of any speaking beings whatsoever" (ibid., 28), genuinely democratic practices are thus characterized as those movements that are able to *articulate* politically the entirety of such subjective instances, going beyond both the institutional codification of citizenship and the weave of mercantile relations. But what does a similar position tell us regarding the forms to confer on political praxis, as well as regarding ways of rethinking the experience of democracy? And how to gain leverage, in this context, on a practical category such as that foreshadowed by the idea of a radical and autonomous "capture of speech" by the excluded? Effectively, the question here is above all a *performative* conception of politics, which identifies its "essence" in the (collective) act of *claiming* in opposition to both formal juridical neutralization and the liberal–mercantile arithmetic of trade. A conception, above all, that insists on the *temporality of the enunciation*, of translation and negotiation, as a medium for the "articulation" of the various subjective claims that emerge from the social fabric (on the fundamental concept of "articulation" see Laclau and Mouffe 1985; Bhabha 1994; Hall 2006a and 2006b; Ong 2006). In this view it seems useful here to recall a suggestive image around which a recent dialogue on belonging, equality, and citizenship was worked out between the two theoreticians Judith Butler and Gayatri Spivak (see Butler and

Spivak 2007). And, specifically, the image of some demonstrations that in the spring of 2006 saw great numbers of "illegal" residents march through the streets of Los Angeles and other Californian cities to the sound of the United States national anthem sung in Spanish. The emergence of *nuestro hymno* introduces, Judith Butler underlines, "the interesting problem of the plurality of the nation, of the 'we' and the 'our': to whom does this anthem belong?" (ibid., 58). But above all it is the very act of singing—an intrinsically plural act, the articulation of a plurality—that questions the sense of "we," and the notions of national equality and belonging. In particular, one part of the anthem sung in the "illegal" language, "*somos equales*," stating in a performative manner the equality in the exercise of freedom, not only installs "the task of translation at the heart of the nation" (ibid., 61), casting light on how "equality" does not mean linearly extending or increasing the homogeneity of a nation or of a social body. But it also shows how both the ontology of liberal individualism and the ideal of a common language are stymied by "a collectivity that comes to exercise its freedom in a language or a set of languages for which difference and translation are irreducible" (ibid., 62).

From these theoretical premises there follows therefore not only a *performative* vision of politics, centered on the "power of speech" of subjects excluded from the perimeter of citizenship on each occasion, and thus contingently, but also a *declarative* conception of rights, which cannot but recall—as its own genetic site and wellspring—the Arendtian idea of an insuppressible "right to rights," the existence of which (and its subsistence) are inseparable from its own uninterrupted declaration and assertion (Arendt 1951; in this regard see above all Benhabib 2004, 59 *et seqq.*). As Balibar writes, "the crucial notion suggested by Arendt, i.e., a 'right to have rights,' does not feature a *minimal* remainder of the political, made of juridical and moral claims to be protected by a constitution; it is much more the idea of a *maximum*. Or, better said, it refers to the continuous process in which a *minimal* recognition of the belonging of human beings to the 'common' sphere of existence [. . .] already involves—and makes possible—a totality of rights"

(Balibar 2004, 119). In this "insurrectional" element of democracy—which brings it back continuously to the originary gesture of claiming (an existence, a belonging, the right to difference)—also lies the medium for its self-realization, which cannot but reside in a logic of *iteration* (Benhabib 2004 and 2006), or, to express it with Chakrabarty and Homi Bhabha, in a logic of *translation*, of negotiation and resignification, through which "universalistic rights principles and collective self-determination claims [. . .] must be renegotiated, reappropriated, and rearticulated" (Benhabib 2004, 115), thus rendered permeable to new and unforeseen semantic contexts. But this constant process of collective resignification—at once a repositioning and rearticulating of rights on the stage of the public sphere—inevitably leads to a conception of collective subjectivity (or of "agency") that acquires its own reality in a *conjunctural* manner, according to the single occurrences of *political articulation* of the differing and multiple subjective and social instances. Nevertheless, such recodification of subjectivity cannot but refer in its turn to a reconfiguration of the insuperable and originary nexus that has always bound politics and ontology: a nexus that today we find eminently and brilliantly reproposed and repositioned within the framework of postcolonial feminist criticism.

6.3. Difference and Position: Alliances Located

The "controversy of the sexes" (Fraisse 2001) constitutes the instance that is at one and the same time the most poignant and the most crystalline of the originary unity of ontology and politics: here, indeed, the fundamental coordinates (and their correlate aporias) regarding the categories of identity and difference, equality and freedom, are found gathered in an inextricable complex that in its entirety is the site of an *aporia*.[1] In this view, the analysis (theoretical and philosophical) of relations between the sexes is captured at its origin at the site of a paradox that involves the point of intersection between ontology (identity/difference) and politics (equality/freedom), keeping itself at the same time at due distance from the strictly anthropological preoccupation of defining—albeit also to criticize it—a presumed "order of the sexes" (see, in this sense, Héritier 1996). Postcolonial feminist criticism (a label applied with a certain degree of inaccuracy to designate the diversified African-American, Chicano or Indian feminisms) has in recent decades played a role as a forceful factor of decentering with regard to some propositions from the constellation of postcolonial studies, as well as with regard to the more or less submerged Eurocentric canon with which academic feminism itself has described itself and its own subjects. The question here, indeed, is not only, in the finest feminist tradition, the assertion of a radical and irreducible "political difference" which, distinct from any "social question," must be understood above all as "eccentric to and additional to universal individualism" (Boccia 2002, 35); but also the failure of the binary codes that have traditionally regulated the debate on relations between the sexes, and the consequent vertiginous multiplication of the axes of differentiation around which today the relations between difference and relationships of dominion are articulated. A multiplication by virtue of which the most traditional notions of gender, body, equality, or *agency* have come to intersect with categories such as caste, community, or religion. From here there has followed not only stringent analysis of the many differentials of power *among* women, but also a reconfiguration—this time strictly epistemological—of key concepts such as "positioning," "agency," and "subjectification." In this perspective, the differences of gender, race and culture have emerged as factors that, far from flanking one another or adding up according to a flatly arithmetic paradigm, constitute themselves as poles which, interacting, do produce new practices of resistance, but also unknown forms of subjection.

Above all it is to Gayatri Spivak that we owe the revelation of the absence, in the field of postcolonial studies in general, and in that of "subaltern studies" in particular, of a thematization of the difference between the sexes—or of the "constitution of the subaltern as (sexed) subject" (Spivak 1988, 29)—and the simultaneous identification in the status of the "Third World woman" of a position of *double subalternization*, or of double negation, by virtue of which "native" women, as well as having been privileged targets of "enlightened" colonial policies, have also played the role of "neglected syntagm of the semiosis of subalternity or insurgency" (ibid., 28). In analysis of the anticolonial insurgencies, "femininity" or the "woman" has indeed been primarily codified as a discursive field, *emblem* of a set (be it religion, the nation, or culture) or, even more so, as a *sign*: wherein the "sign," according to the teachings of Claude Lévi-Strauss (Lévi-Strauss 1947), is always the vehicle and the site of an *exchange* of meaning. This condition of doubled subalternity—or of *forclusion*—of the "native" woman is reduplicated, as mentioned, in relations with much of European and American feminism, for which the "Third World woman" is often raised to an archetypal figure of "universal victim" and as index of an irrecuperable historical delay compared to the Western destinies of emancipation. It is in this sense that Spivak urges the location "of feminist individualism in its historical determination rather than simply to canonize it as feminism as such" (Spivak 1999, 116), and at the same time she urges us to look at the "pattern of resistance among these 'permanent casuals' " and the "heterogeneous subject-constitution of the subaltern female" (Spivak 1988, 29). But it is in particular to the excavation work carried out by Chandra Talpade Mohanty on the tacit Eurocentric assumptions operating in the international feminist canon that we owe the clearest exposition of the exquisitely theoretical stakes played by postcolonial feminism. In a well-known essay by the title "Under Western Eyes: Feminist Scholarship and Colonial Discourse" (1984), Mohanty indeed had identified at the basis of the production of the "average Third World woman"—as singular and monolithic subject correlate of the politics of "development" and of "civilization"—the operation of some strategies of discursive colonization aimed at the suppression of the material and historical *heterogeneity* of the lives of the women in question. More specifically, Mohanty had illuminated in an effective manner how the application of presumed *transcultural universals* (in the first instance a monolithic notion of patriarchy and male domination) was functional to the production of an ahistorical and universal unity among women constructed on the basis of a generalized notion of their subordination, or of a sort of forced "commonality in oppression" (see Mohanty 2003, 17 *et seqq.*).

From this point of view, the concept of "gender"—and here we assume its hermeneutic validity with as point of departure the definition offered by Joan Scott as "social organization of sexual difference" (Scott 1999, 2)—which is habitually located in the rubric "individual-rights-identity-equality," appears marked and furrowed by a hegemonic reading that limits its range of questioning and radically fixes its terms: above all in the extent to which it finds itself being articulated beginning with an all-encompassing notion of "patriarchy," which in its turn presupposes (and involuntarily legitimizes) the existence of a closed and monolithic system of relations of dominion. It is in this sense that it becomes necessary and useful to look not just at the historical and cultural variations of patriarchal relations, but also at the various semantic implications deriving from the concept of "gender" according to context and epoch or, better still, to look at all those *semantic drifts* that radically widen the concept's matrix, posing the crucial problem of cultural translation. As was opportunely brought to light by Seemanthini Niranjana, careful attention directed at the "incarnate" body and at female "agency" allows us to look at the plural and diversified *matrices (socio-spatial) of sexualization* inherent to each culture: in other words, to direct the gaze to the specific sites (material and symbolic) of *subjectification* periodically formed by the interface between the material body of the woman, the body of cultural representation, and the different modalities with which women experience such constitutive conditions of their identity (see Niranjana 2001 and 2004). In measures widely testified to with a growing number of controversies throughout contemporary societies, women's bodies (veiled bodies, bare bodies, mutilated or asserted bodies) are constantly lived and represented in convergence with other narratives (such as narratives of community, of nation, of morality, or of religion), in such a way that a reckoning of the female experience and "incarnation" cannot but take into account the variability of cultural beliefs and practices, of the norms and codes of regulation, which repeatedly locate female difference and agency in an intermediate zone between substance and discourse, or between "material" and "cultural." Spivak writes:

> The body, like all other things, cannot be thought, as such. I take the extreme ecological view that the body as such has no possible outline. As body it is a repetition of nature. It is in the rupture with Nature when it is a signifier of immediacy for the staging of the self. As a text, the inside of the body (imbricated with the outside) is mysterious and unreadable except by way of thinking of the systematicity of the body, value coding of the body. It is through the *significance* of my body and others' bodies that cultures become gendered, economico-politic, selved, substantive. (Spivak 1993d, 20)

Taking a transversal view with regard to the long-lasting (and often sterile) discussion on the opposition between "gender" and "sexual difference," postcolonial feminism thus gives priority to a *resemanticization* of the very notion of "gender," with a *dynamic* and *processual* conception of difference as point of departure. Indeed, there is no single answer to the question, rendered essential by the work of Judith Butler (Butler 1990, 1993 and 2004a): *is* one a gender, does one *belong* to a gender, or does one *become* a gender? If the body, as Spivak writes, "cannot be thought, as such," and if, on the other hand, it is precisely the body that has constituted the grand text of the essentialism on the form of which the essence of Woman has been read by "phallocentrism," postcolonial feminist criticism takes a side road, breaking ranks both with biological essentialism and with a facile form of cultural constructivism.[2] In this context it is to the *historicity* (of contexts and relations) that the function of relieving the tensions inherent to the dichotomic and binary representations of the relation history/nature is delegated. In such representations nature, when invoked in the political register, always functions to translate and re-transcribe history into Nature, demonstrating how a presumed naturalness (of bodies and of genders) is inherent to the very production (Eurocentric and phallocentric) of history (on logocentric and phallocentric recourse to historical figurations of the female body as metaphors of a radically de-corporealized, or disincarnate "political," see Cavarero 2002). According to a trend that can be found within what is called *third wave feminism*, the body is thus here neither the site of an immutable essence subtracted from sociocultural codes, nor a virgin receptacle or a "volume in perpetual disintegration" as Foucault wrote in "Nietzsche, Genealogy and History" (1971), pointing to "a body totally imprinted by history and the process of history's destruction of the body" (Foucault 1977b, 148). It is rather reinscribed as a *site of incarnation* or, to use the words of Rosi Braidotti, as a surface of signification "situated at the intersection of the alleged facticity of anatomy with the symbolic dimension of language" (Braidotti 2011, 127). In other words: the grammar of gender, being neither biological nor cultural, is configured as a constant and uninterrupted *process of symbolization of the human*, understanding which requires above all recognition of the fundamental historicity of the ties (real and imaginary) between the sexes.

Within this profile, embracing Niranjana's proposal to operate a cartography of the various "matrices of sexualization" of cultures allows us to articulate the question of "incarnation" from the point of view of the tie between the body and female agency: and this to the extent to which attention in the first instance is focused on the *historic sites of subjectification* in which the singularity and the difference of women is inscribed. Postcolonial feminist criticism, insisting on the *heterogeneity* of the historical experience and the positioning of women with respect to the principal coordinates of power (first above all, the public/private partition), has indeed at the same time demonstrated how the female body has been—and continues to be—the fundamental operator in the institution of the *frontiers* between communities and within each community. The Chinese theoretician Rey Chow, in a fertile analysis of the controversial chapters that Frantz Fanon dedicated in *Peau noire, masques blanches* to "femininity," has after all effectively brought to light how every thematization of the *community* is always by implication a theory on *reproduction* (social and biological) within which the particular female sexual agency—as power of reproduction, of contagion, of transmission and confusion of bodies—fractures the social order in the most essential way (but on female sexual agency as power of confusion of bodies see also Braidotti 1996):

> Women, because they have the capability of embodying physical contact—of giving material form to "touching," to the transgression of bodily boundaries—in the form of reproduction, are always potentially dangerous. [. . .] What dangers does a *female* tendency toward miscegenation hold for a theory of community formation in the aftermath of colonialism? (Chow 2010, 62 and 69)

On her part over the years Spivak has put forward a deconstruction of the Marxian theory of value introducing into it the parameter of sexuality, or better, the figure itself of the woman as a continuous resource of *surplus value*: "the possession of a tangible place of reproduction, the womb, situates women as agents in any theory of production" (Spivak 1985, 57; see also Spivak 2008, 253). But such redefinitions of female agency as, literally, figure of a productive "intercommunitary contagion" have their roots in a precise epistemological declension of the category of "location" and in a vision that is, yes, contextual, but is not contextualist, of the notion of "difference." The very concept of "location"—elaborated in the first instance on the epistemological plane to escape from the paralyzing alternative of universalism and relativism (see Harding 1998 and Harding, ed. 2004)—indeed refers to a *located* conception of the subject and of knowledge, the counterpart of which is a "partial" vision of the basis of the perspective on which political coalitions and alliances can be built. As Donna Haraway has written: "Location is not a listing of adjectives or assigning of labels such as race, sex, and class. Location is not the concrete to the abstract of decontextualization. Location is the always partial, always finite, always fraught play of foreground and background, text and context, that constitutes critical inquiry. Above all, location is not self-evident or transparent" (Haraway 1997, 37). If the "location," rather than being a given, represents an objective for which subjects and groups have to struggle, then there follows an "intersectional" conception (on the category of intersectionality, see Crenshaw 1989 and 1995) that is eccentric to difference and for which a simultaneous but distinct series of axes of subjectification (gender, class, ethnic origin) is analyzed in its constant and unpredictable interaction. On this critical paradigm centered on the ineradicable localization of the discourses and structures of subjectivity, the postcolonial view confers a geopolitical coloring that modifies and sharpens its contours: here, indeed, the multiplication of the axes of differentiation that structure subjective identity is accompanied by a concomitant remodulation and redefinition of agency (or of social action) in relation to the concrete historical–material dynamics of political subjectification or, to use Judith Butler's words, in relation to the unequal "geopolitical distribution of corporeal vulnerability" (Butler 2004b, 29) and the possible potential of "resistance" and "liberation" that follows from it. Think, for example, of the forms assumed by the present-day "globalization" of female work, by virtue of which the transfer to the global scale of the "traditional" functions associated with the female role—from the tasks of caring for children and the elderly to the much grimmer condition of sex worker—from the North to the South of the world is accompanied on the one hand by trajectories of redemption and liberation and on the other by a condition of clandestinity and invisibility that erases the women in question (see Ehrenreich and Hochschild, eds. 2003).

The "hierarchy of grief" (Butler 2004b, 32) that marks the geopolitically differentiated relations among women leads therefore to a requestioning of the relation between "dehumanization" and "discourse" (or, Foucauldianly, "discursive formation") that renders the location-as-subject, or the enunciative location, of women (plural) not so much a datum to be essentialized, as an objective to be defended or earned. In this view, it is the work of a theoretician of the likes of Judith Butler that offers important coordinates for a redefinition of the category of "location" and, consequently, the very notion of "gender": wherein gender is reinterpreted as "an improvisational possibility within a field of constraints" (Butler

2004a, 15). The stress here, indeed, should be placed not so much on the term "improvisational" (in line with criticism often leveled at Butler's work), as rather on the question of the *constraints*, not only structural but *historical*, which govern the assumption of the gender and the status of a "visible" subject:

> Whose life is counted as a life? Whose prerogative is it to live? How do we decide when life begins and ends, and how do we think life against life? Under what conditions should life come into being, and through what means? [. . .] And to what extent does gender, coherent gender, secure a life as livable? What threat of death is delivered to those who do not live gender according to its accepted norms? (ibid., 205)

Although Butler's questions underpin above all a denouncement of the implicit "heterosexual contract" that regulates much of mainstream academic feminism, the attention paid to the matter of *norms* and *normativity* as privileged site of power in which a *differential production of the human* is effected corresponds to the effort made by postcolonial feminism itself to question again the standards of normalization implicated by the assumption of a privileged group (the "white-Western-heterosexual-woman," for example) as exclusive referent in the field of social practice. Normativity, indeed, is deployed—Butler reminds us—above all as the production of a series of grids of legibility (morphological, racial, sexual grids) that mark at the same time the boundaries of cultural intelligibility: which is to say the boundaries of that which has value as "human" and as "less than human" or, even worse, as "inhuman" (see Butler 2004a and 2004b). Nevertheless, where Butler proposes—faced with the differential production of that which has value as "human" or "less than human"—a thinking of "performativity" conceived of as *subjective* reiteration and resignification of cultural norms, part of postcolonial feminist criticism (embodied in theoreticians such as Vandana Shiva or Gayatri Spivak herself: see Shiva 2005) projects its own analysis over a global surface or, even better, a *planetary* surface. Here the "planet" becomes the prominent figure of alterity and responsibility, and with this it also becomes the extreme that is the point of departure for reflection on "subalternity":

> To be human is to be intended toward the other. We provide for ourselves transcendental figurations of what we think is the origin of this animating gift: mother, nation, god, nature. These are the names of alterity, some more radical than others. Planet-thought opens up to embrace an inexhaustible taxonomy of such names, including but not identical with the whole range of human universals: aboriginal animism as well as the spectral white mythology of postrational science. If we imagine ourselves as planetary subjects rather than global agents, planetary creatures rather than global entities, alterity remains underived from us; it is not our dialectical negation, it contains us as much as it flings us away. (Spivak 2003a)

The imperative to "re-imagine the planet," indeed, involves the visualization of a "planetary subject," which with its bare life exposed to the world, exists without an already pre-established cartography: a subject whose debt, not being payable to nature (or to the "mother" as Spivak puts it, echoing Melanie Klein), is payable as *responsibility* toward others. Toward, above all, those others and those collectivities whose state of subalternity postcolonial criticism (and feminist postcolonial criticism in particular) sets out to overturn:

> The "planet" is, here, as perhaps always, a catachresis for inscribing collective responsibility as right. Its alterity, determining experience, is mysterious and discontinuous—an experience of the impossible. It is such collectivities that must be opened up with the question "How many are we?" when cultural origin is detranscendentalized into fiction—the toughest task in the diaspora. (Spivak 2003a)

Notes

Foreword

1. If one takes the care to reconnect the modern concept of subject not so much to a grammatical *subjectum* as to a juridical–political *subjectus* or *subditus*.

2. Here I signal the fine pages Emanuela Fornari dedicates to the "aporias of memory," with specific reference to the concepts of Michel de Certeau.

3. This is without a doubt one of the reasons that explain the renewed contemporary and suggestive power of the work of Fanon, thinker par excellence of this finitude, to whom, along the lines of her authors of reference, in particular Edward Said, Emanuela Fornari never ceases to return.

4. The construction of this conceptual reciprocity between "translation" and "transition," by means of a juxtaposition within postcolonial criticism of the uniforming codes of the capitalist West and the interpretation of "minority writings," put forward by Deleuze and Guattari, constitutes one of the philosophical *tours de force* of Emanuela Fornari's book.

Chapter 1

1. For obvious reasons it is not possible here to give a full account of the endless debate produced—even merely in terms of philosophical and critical–cultural reflection—around the lemma "globalization." For a theoretical framing, not far from the perspective adopted here and centered on the strict interrelation between the "symbolic" dimension

and the "material" dimension, reference is made, however, principally to Appadurai, ed. 2001; Jameson and Miyoshi, eds. 1998; Marramao 2012. An analysis focalized specifically on the transformations of the "political space" caused by the passage from the modern era to the global era is to be found instead in Galli 2001.

2. Useful introductions to the field of postcolonial studies are to be found in, among others, Ashcroft, Griffiths and Tiffin, eds. 1995; Chambers and Curti, eds. 1996; Loomba 1998; Young 1990, 2001, 2003; and, in the Italian sphere, in Albertazzi and Vecchi, eds. 2004; Cometa 2004; Mellino 2005. A recent and effective critical reconstruction of the "postcolonial paradigm" that while recognizing in it an effective discussion of western philosophy as "metanarrative of the origin" and highlights the possible relativist and "indigenist" outcomes, is to be found in Amselle 2008.

3. The Subaltern Studies Collective consists of a group of Indian historians (including Ranajit Guha, Partha Chatterjee, Sumit Sarkar, and Dipesh Chakrabarty) who, beginning in the 1980s, have worked at the revision of the historiography of colonial and postcolonial India in the direction of a liberation both from the elitist paradigm that denied any authentic "political" role to the peasants of the countryside in the conquest of independence from British domination and from a strictly Marxist paradigm centered on the "grand narrative" of the means of production (see below, part one, chapter 2). Between 1982 and 2000 eleven volumes of *Subaltern Studies* were published, of which the first ten by Oxford University Press and the eleventh by Columbia University Press. Anthological selections of the main texts produced by the group are found in Guha and Spivak, eds. 1988 and in Guha 1997. A volume that deals thoroughly with the entire experience (not lacking in turns and disagreements) of Subaltern Studies is Chaturvedi, ed. 2000.

4. See de Certeau 1988, 90–91: "The narrative [. . .] marks this initial and unassignable reference, the absolute condition for any possibility of its historicization, on the entire surface of its organization. By allowing the present to be "situated" in time and, finally, to be symbolized, narrative posits it within a necessary relation to a "beginning" which is *nothing*, or which serves merely as a limit. The anchoring of the narrative conveys everywhere a tacit relation to something which cannot have a place in history—an originary non-place—without which, however, there would be no historiography."

5. Regarding the crucial nature of the dimension of *writing* as discriminating factor between the "civilized space" and the "barbarous

space," the reference is obviously to the works of Derrida, to whom Guha himself turns in his critique of the Hegelian scheme: see in particular Derrida 1967 and 1972. After all, the notion of "people without a State," from the ethnological point of view, cannot but lead to the celebrated analyses of Pierre Clastres (1974).

6. Regarding this see also Chatterjee 1993, for example p. 5: "If nationalisms in the rest of the world have to choose their imagined community from certain 'modular' forms already made available to them by Europe and the Americas, what do they have left to imagine? History, it would seem, has decreed that we in the postcolonial world shall only be perpetual consumers of modernity. Europe and the Americas, the only true subjects of history, have thought out on our behalf not only the script of colonial enlightenment and exploitation, but also that of our anticolonial resistance and postcolonial misery. Even our imaginations must remain forever colonized."

7. Alessandro Dal Lago and Sandro Mezzadra quite rightly remark on the difference between the terms "boundary" and "border," even although they are semantically contiguous. Indeed, whereas the former, from its original indication of spatial limits, refers to the act of *instituting* a line of division, the latter indicates rather a *relational* movement of transition (see Dal Lago and Mezzadra 2002, 143). It should also be remembered that in the French language the semantic spaces affected by the two terms are inverted with regard to the Italian language: the Italian term *confine* indeed corresponds to the French *frontière*, while the Italian *frontiera* instead finds its semantic equivalent in the French *confin*. One of the intentions of this chapter, nevertheless, is precisely that of bringing to light the impossibility of a similar clear semantic distinction, beginning with the undecidability of a gesture of *partage* as being at the same time "division" and "con-division."

8. Balibar indeed remarks that "if there is now a new discourse (but is it so new after all?) on the *end of the nations*, it is because there is already and more than ever a discourse on the *origin of the nations*." A discourse, i.e., on the limits and the particularities inherent to the European conception of historicity, of identity, of political violence and action, strictly related to—if not dependent on—the very concept of nation (see Balibar 2004, 15).

9. Balibar writes: "Borders are vacillating. This does not mean that they are disappearing. Less than ever is the contemporary world a "world without borders." On the contrary, borders are being both multiplied and

reduced in their localization and their function; they are being thinned out and doubled, becoming borders *zones, regions,* or *countries* where one can reside and live. The quantitative relation between "border" and "territory" is being inverted." (Balibar 2002, 92.) After all, just above this Balibar remarked significantly: "This vacillation affects our very consciousness of a European "identity," because Europe is the point in the world whence border lines set forth to be drawn throughout the world, because it is the native land of the very representation of the border as this sensible and supersensible "thing" that should *be* or *not be,* be *here* or *there,* a bit beyond (*jenseits*) or short of (*diesseits*) its ideal "position," but always *somewhere*" (ibid., 88).

Chapter 2

1. The concept of "foreclosure" used by Spivak (a concept matured from Lacan's lexis that translates with this lemma the Freudian *Verwerfung*), indicates that rejection of a fundamental signifier outside of the symbolic universe of the subject, which is also an *immediate rejection in the exterior.* In other terms, "foreclosure" consists in "not symbolising what ought to be symbolised": it is, according to the compendium provided by Laplanche and Pontalis, a radical "symbolic abolition" (Laplanche and Pontalis 1988, 168). Following a line of enquiry from a reference to the indigenous peoples of the Tierra del Fuego in Kant's *Critique of Judgment,* Spivak puts forward as a striking example the way in which the very noumenic construction is based on a foreclosure/rejection of the "aborigine" or, put another way, the narrative contained in "Analytic of the Sublime" on the necessary transition from Nature to Culture through the feeling of the sublime is part of a story that codifies a *limited access to the human.* The introduction, in Kant's text on the sublime, of the "uneducated man" as a denied foundation of the transcendental subject is not indeed limited to marking the irreducibility of the *anthropological moment* in Kant, but also underlines how right there where the normative foundations of theoretical reason are brought to light, there emerges an insurmountable contamination of the empirical that is part and parcel with the structures of a "geopolitically differentiated" humanism (see Spivak 1999, 35 *et seqq.*).

2. But then again, regarding the emergence of a principle of historiographical objectification based on the sense of the *anachronism*

as origin of the *historical consciousness* of modernity, by virtue of which the "historical evidence" (or the "archive") is made to coincide with the faculty of qualifying a contemporary phenomenon as *residue* or *remains* of another time or of another place, see Chakrabarty 2000, 238.

3. Nicole Loraux, historian of the classical period, in maintaining that for the historian it is necessary to grant space to the phenomena of repetition along the axis of the chronological time of history, significantly justifies this *attention for the repetitive* with a "systematic taking into consideration the passions and the relationship with power" (Loraux 1993, 36).

Chapter 3

1. The list of critical works on this text is now endless, but worthy of note is Michael Löwy's essay, "Walter Benjamin: Avvertissement d'incendie. Une lecture des thèses 'sur le concept d'histoire,'" in which the author undertakes a re-reading of Benjamin's theses, interweaving them with various historical and political instances of struggle in the second half of the twentieth century (from the British "history from below," to women's history, to the Latin American experience), in the firm conviction that "through the prism of a determinate historic moment" Benjamin had raised "questions that bear on the whole of modern history and on the place of the twentieth century in the social development of humanity" (Löwy 2005, 19).

2. In the cabalistic and messianic echo of this *restitutio* (condensed enigmatically in Thesis IX with the expression "make whole what has been smashed" [*das Zerschlagene zusammenfügen*]), which recalls the *tiqqûn* of the Lurianic Kabbalah, as messianic restitution of the original state of divine harmony shattered by the *shevirat ha-kelim* (the "breaking of the vessels") following the original "contraction" or "withdrawal" of God (*zimzûm*), see in particular the pages that Gershom Scholem dedicates to the topic in Scholem 1972.

3. On how this strength of the "symbol"—or of the *Bild* as opposed to the *Ideal*—completely rooted in the past, constitutes a form of "messianism without delay," see Marramao 2008, 108 *et seqq*.

4. It is worthwhile quoting here in its entirety the passage in which Ricoeur justifies the legitimacy of the application of psychoanalytic categories within historical–social fields: "It is the bipolar constitution of personal and community identity that, ultimately, justifies extending the Freudian

analysis of mourning to the traumatisation of collective identity. We can speak not only in an analogical sense but in terms of a direct analysis of collective traumatisms, of wounds to collective memory [. . .] The transposition of pathological categories to the historical plane would be more completely justified if we were able to show that it applies not only to the exceptional situations [. . .] but that these depend on a fundamental structure of collective existence. What I refer to here is the fundamental relation of history to violence" (Ricoeur 2004, 78–79). Note also how Jean-François Lyotard makes reference to Freud's 1914 essay as a paradigm for a *re-writing of modernity* beyond the "postmodern" in Lyotard 1988.

Chapter 4

1. On the structural and unresolvable tension between "translatability" and "untranslatability"—by virtue of which "the pure transferable can announce itself, give itself, present itself, let itself be translated *as untranslatable*"—see the Derridean reading of Benjamin's essay in Derrida 1985 (p. 203).

Chapter 5

1. It is worth recalling how Clifford's work (1988 and 1997) has its theoretical roots in the book—a veritable watershed in U.S. disciplinary vicissitudes regarding anthropology, cultural studies and so forth—edited together with George E. Marcus, *Writing Culture* (Clifford and Marcus, eds. 1986): here, contesting "an ideology claiming transparency of representation and immediacy of experience" (ibid. 2) and acknowledging various instances ascribable to that which in the widest sense might be defined as "poststructuralism," the authors put forward an intimately *conflictual* conception of "culture" as "composed of seriously contested codes and representations" (ibid.), which, immersed in historical and linguistic processes, can only be understood as a constant and uninterrupted "interplay of voices, of positioned utterances" (ibid. 12).

2. On the indissoluble link, one might say the ontological link, that binds identity and power, the words dedicated to the subject in a now classic volume with the significant title, *Contro l'identità* [*Against Identity*] by Francesco Remotti are worthy of consideration: "As a product of an

effort in differentiation, it [identity] also involves a strength, a power and in some way the exercise of a violence: ties are broken, connections are interrupted in order to give rise to the constructions of identity; and the subjects of identity manifest in this way their strength, their power" (Remotti 2001, 9–10).

3. The category of "hybridization" (often superimposed on the category "métissage") has for some time been at the center of a wide-ranging critical debate in ethno-anthropological thought regarding the category of "ethnicity," the political–ideological origins of which can be traced back to colonial procedures of "classification" and the correlated devices of abstraction of subjects and groups by the sociocultural *continuum*: see, in this regard, Amselle and M'Bokolo 1985 and Amselle 1990 in particular, as well as (in praise of *métissage*), Laplantine 1999. For an articulated critique, from the points of view of various disciplines, of the concept of "hybridization" in the field of cultural studies, see Brah and Coombes 2000.

4. The notion of "mimicry," contiguous with the category of "masquerade," was at the center of an intense debate within not only postcolonial but also feminist thought: on the category of "masquerade," coined by the psychoanalyst Joan Rivière in 1929 in reading female identity, see in particular Rivière 1929, Heath 1986, and Doane 1991a and 1991b.

5. For an illuminating study on the slangs of the "criminal classes" and, in particular, of Parisian *argot* as a linguistic phenomenon that lays bare the inadequacy of the theoretical instruments of linguists and etymologists, see Becker-Ho 2015: "In argot words are weapons that can be loaded and unloaded at leisure, as circumstances dictate. They "give cover," or give the signal, inform or disinform, amuse or threaten. Argot is *the power of those words that constantly remind us that it is dangerous to talk*: sometimes too much, sometimes not enough. [. . .] Slang is the truth of man. It is the very core of the human spirit struggling also with its language" (66).

6. See in this regard the inspiring chapter that Adriana Cavarero dedicates to Brathwaite's poetry in Cavarero 2005 (chapter 6, "The Hurricane Does Not Roar in Pentameter"), where we read how the originary languages of the Africans deported to the Caribbean "have acted like a hidden language, capable of modifying English and of undermining the cultural imperative of European languages. [. . .] Caribbean poetry—and, more generally all poetry in which an African voice vibrates—bends the dominant language to a vocalic that is at once direct experience of the environment and memory of the lost world" (ibid., 147 and 149).

7. On the strategic role within postcolonial literary studies of "writing back," see Ashcroft, Griffiths, and Tiffin, eds. 1989. But see also Toni Morrison's fine essay on the African presence in American literature, where the "black," apparently only an "ornamental vacuum," constitutes—through specific literary strategies of occultation and shifting—the very driving force of the construction of the ideology of whiteness (Morrison 1992).

8. But on the impossibility of "monolingualism" see above all Derrida 1998, in which the author not only ties the originary structure of alienation from language (by which it is possible to say, "I have but one language—yet that language is not mine.") to the situation of colonial alienation—and to his own condition of Algerian Jew deprived of French citizenship following the Vichy emergency laws of 1942. But he also explores the relationship between the figure of the mother and language, regarding the necessity/impossibility of the "mother tongue" (ibid. 89). For a reading of Defoe's novel that is completely in line with postcolonial interpretations, in which Friday demonstrates that "*le corps est l'autre qui fait parler, mais qu'on ne fait pas parler*," see de Certeau 1986, 215–18.

Chapter 6

1. The notion of "controversy," inferred from the works of Geneviève Fraisse (1996, 2001, and 2004), like the concept of "aporia," or again, Jacques Rancière's *point de mésentente* [point of disagreement], forestalls in our opinion any essentializing gesture, indicating rather the in-finity of the "conflict" between the sexes.

2. An important consideration of the debate on the essentialism/anti-essentialism dyad, which has occupied much of international feminism in recent decades, is to be found in Fuss 1989. Here the author argues the theoretical impossibility of a radically anti-essentialistic position. Regarding the category "strategic essentialism"—conceived of not so much as a middle ground between the two poles of essentialism and anti-essentialism, but rather as a *located practice* of identities—see, for a general overview, Rajchman, ed. 1995.

Bibliography

Accarino, B. 1999. *Rappresentanza*. Bologna: Il Mulino.
Adamo, S. 2007. "La traduzione come metafora concettuale." In *Culture planetarie? Prospettive e limiti della teoria e della critica culturale*, edited by S. Adamo, 193–211. Rome: Meltemi.
Agamben, G. 2005. *State of Exception*. Translated by K. Attell. Chicago: University of Chicago Press.
Ahmad, A. 1992. *In Theroy: Classes, Nations, Literatures*. London and New York: Verso.
Albertazzi, S., and R. Vecchi, eds. 2004. *Abbecedario postcoloniale I–II. Venti voci per un lessico della postcolonialità*. Macerata: Quodlibet.
Amselle, J.-L. 1990. *Logiques métisses. Anthropologie de l'identité en Afrique et ailleurs*. Paris: Éditions Payot.
———. 2008. *L'Occident décroché. Enquête sur les postcolonialismes*. Paris: Éditions Stock.
Amselle, J.-L., and E. M'Bokolo. 1985. *Au coeur de l'ethnie*. Paris: Éditions La Découverte.
Anderson, B. 1983. *Imagined Communities. Reflections on the Origin and Spread of Nationalism*. London and New York: Verso.
Anzaldúa, G. 1987. *Borderlands/La Frontera: The New Mestiza*. San Francisco: Aunt Lute.
Appadurai, A., 1996. *Modernity at Large: Cultural Dimensions of Globalization*. Minneapolis and London: University of Minnesota Press.
———, ed. 2001. *Globalization*. Durham, NC, and London: Duke University Press.
———. 2006. *Fear of Small Numbers. An Essay on the Geography of Anger*. Durham, NC, and London. Duke University Press.

Arendt, H. 1951. *The Origins of Totalitarianism*. New York: Harcourt Brace.
———. 1968. "Walter Benjamin, 1892-1940." In W. Benjamin 1968: 1–58.
Ashcroft, B., G. Griffiths, and H. Tiffin, eds. 1989. *The Empire Writes Back: Theory and Practice in Postcolonial Literatures*. London and New York: Routledge.
———, eds. 1995. *The Post-Colonial Reader*. London and New York: Routledge.
Augé, M. 1992. *Non-lieux. Introduction à une anthropologie de la surmodernité*. Paris: Seuil.
———. 2003. *Le Temps en ruines*. Paris: Galilée.
Bakhtin, M. 1981. *The Dialogic Imagination*. Edited by M. Holquist, translated by C. Emerson and M. Holquist, Austin, TX, and London: University of Texas Press.
Balibar, É. 1994. "Subjection and Subjectivation." In Copjec ed. 2004: 1–15.
———. 1995. *The Philosophy of Marx*. Translated by G. Elliott and Ch. Turner. London and New York: Verso.
———. 1997. *La Crainte des masses. Politique et philosophie avant et après Marx*. Paris: Galilée.
———. 2002. *Politics and the Other Scene*. Translated by Ch. Jones, J. Swenson, and Ch. Turner. London and New York: Verso.
———. 2003. *L'Europe, l'Amérique, la guerre. Réflexions sur la médiation européenne*. Paris: Éditions La Découverte.
———. 2004. *We, the People of Europe? Reflections on Transnational Citizenship*. Translated by J. Swenson. Princeton, NJ, and Oxford: Princeton University Press.
———. 2005. *Europe Constitution Frontière*. Bègles: Éditions du Passant.
———. 2006a. "Sub specie universitatis." *Topoi* 25(1/2): 3–16.
———. 2006b. "Strangers as Enemies: Further Reflections on the Aporias of Transnational Citizenship." *Globalization Working Paper* 06/4. Institute on Globalization and the Human Condition, McMaster University.
———. 2007. "Uprisings in the Banlieues." *Constellations* 14(1): 47–71.
———. 2009. "Europe as borderland." *Environment and Planning D: Society and Space* 27: 190–215.
Bassnett, S., and H. Trivedi. 1999. *Postcolonial Translation. Theory and Practice*. London and New York: Routledge.
Bauman, Z. 2004. *Wasted Lives. Modernity and its Outcasts*. Cambridge and Oxford, UK: Polity Press-Blackwell.

Becker-Ho, A. 2015. *The Essence of Jargon: Argot and the Dangerous Classes*. Translated by J. McHale, New York: Autonomedia.

bell hooks (Gloria Jean Watkins). 1990. *Yearning: Race, Gender, and Cultural Politics*. Boston: South End Press.

Benhabib, S. 2002. *The Claims of Culture: Equality and Diversity in the Global Era*. Princeton, NJ: Princeton University Press.

———. 2004. *The Rights of Others. Aliens, Residents and Citizens*. Cambridge: Cambridge University Press.

———. 2006. *Another Cosmopolitanism*. Oxford: Oxford University Press.

Benjamin, W. 1968. *Illuminations. Essays and Reflections*. Translated by H. Zohn. Edited by H. Arendt. New York: Harcourt, Brace & World.

———. 1979a. "Über den Begriff der Geschichte." In *Gesammelte Schriften*. Bd. I. T. 2: 691–704. Frankfurt am Main: Suhrkamp.

———. 1979b. "Anmerkungen zu Benjamins *Über den Begriff der Geschichte*." In *Gesammelte Schriften*. Bd. I. T. 3: 1223–266. Frankfurt am Main: Suhrkamp.

———. 2003. "On the Concept of History." In *Selected Writings. Vol. 4, 1938–1940*, translated by E. Jephcott and Others, edited by H. Eiland and M. W. Jennings, Cambridge, MA, and London: Harvard University Press.

Bensaïd, D. 2007. *Les Dépossédés. Karl Marx, les voleurs des bois et le droit des pauvres*. Paris: La fabrique éditions.

Berman, A. 1999. *La Traduction et la lettre ou l'Auberge du lointain*. Paris: Seuil.

Beverley, J. 1989. "The Margin at the Centre: On 'Testimonio' (Testimonial Narrative)." *Modern Fiction Studies* 35(1): 11–28.

Beverley, J., and M. Zimmerman. 1990. *Literature and Politics in the Central American Revolutions*. Austin: University of Texas.

Bhabha, H., 1990. "The Third Space: Interview with Homi Bhabha." In *Identity, Community, Culture, Difference*, edited by J. Rutherford, 207–21. London: Lawrence & Wishart.

———, ed. 1990. *Nation and Narration*. London and New York: Routledge.

———. 1994. *The Location of Culture*. London and New York: Routledge.

———. 1995. "Freedom's Basis in the Indeterminate." In Rajchman, ed. 1995:47–61.

Blanchard, P., N. Bancel, N., and S. Lemaire, eds. 2005. *La Fracture coloniale. La société française au prisme de l'héritage colonial*. Paris: Éditions La Découverte.

Boccia, M. L. 2002. *La differenza politica. Donne e cittadinanza*. Milan: Il Saggiatore.

Brah, A., and A. E. Coombes. 2000. *Hybridity and its Discontents. Politics, Science, Culture.* London and New York: Routledge.

Braidotti, R. 1996. *Madri, mostri e macchine.* Rome: Manifestolibri.

———. 2006. *Transpositions: On Nomadic Ethics.* Cambridge, UK: Polity Press.

———. 2011. *Nomadic Subjects: Embodiment and Sexual Difference in Contemporary Feminist Theory.* 2nd edition. New York: Columbia University Press.

Brathwaite, E. K. 1984. *History of the Voice: The Development of National Language in Anglophone Caribbean Poetry.* London: New Beacon Books.

Butler, J. 1990. *Gender Trouble. Feminism and the Subversion of Identity.* London and New York: Routledge.

———. 1993. *Bodies that Matter. On the Discursive Limits of "Sex."* London and New York: Routledge.

———. 1997. *The Psychic Life of Power. Theories in Subjection.* Stanford, CA: Stanford University Press.

———. 2000. "Restaging the Universal: Hegemony and the Limits of Formalism." In Butler, Laclau, and Žižek, 2000:11–43.

———. 2004a. *Undoing Gender.* London and New York: Routledge.

———. 2004b. *Precarious Life. The Powers of Mourning and Violence.* London and New York: Verso.

Butler, J., E. Laclau, and S. Žižek. 2000. *Contingency, Hegemony, Universality. Contemporary Dialogues on the Left.* London and New York: Verso.

Butler, J., and G. Ch. Spivak. 2007. *Who Sings the Nation-State? Language, Politics, Belonging.* London, New York, and Calcutta: Seagull Books.

Butler, J., and J. W. Scott, eds. 1992. *Feminists Theorize the Political.* London and New York: Routledge.

Canclini, N. G. 1990. *Culturas híbridas. Estrategías para entrar y salir de la modernidad.* México: Editorial Grijalbo.

Carravetta, P. 2009. *Del postmoderno. Critica e cultura in America all'alba del Duemila.* Milan: Bompiani.

Cavarero, A. 2002. *Stately Bodies. Literature, Philosophy, and the Question of Gender.* Translated by R. de Lucca and D. Shemek. Ann Arbor, MI: University of Michigan Press.

———. 2005. *For More than One Voice: Toward a Philosophy of Vocal Expression.* Translated by P. A. Kottman. Stanford, CA: Stanford University Press.

Certeau, M. de. 1984. *The Practice of Everyday Life*. Translated by S. Rendall. Berkeley and Los Angeles, CA, London: University of California Press.
———. 1986. *Histoire et psychanalise entre science et fiction*. Paris: Gallimard.
———. 1988. *The Writing of History*. Translated by T. Conley. New York: Columbia University Press.
———. 1997. The *Capture* of *Speech and Other Political Writings*. Translated by T. Conley, edited by L. Giard. Minneapolis: University of Minnesota Press.
Chakrabarty, D. 2000. *Provincializing Europe. Postcolonial Thought and Historical Difference*. Princeton, NJ: Princeton University Press.
———. 2002. *Habitations of Modernity. Essays in the Wake of Subaltern Studies*. Chicago and London: University of Chicago Press.
———. 2003. "Globalization, Democratization and the Evacuation of History?" In *At Home in Diaspora. South Asian Scholars and the West*, edited by J. Assayag and V. Bénéï, 127–47. Bloomington and Indianapolis: Indiana University Press.
———. 2004. "La storia subalterna come pensiero politico." In *Studi culturali* 1(2): 233–52.
———. 2005. "After History. Vergangenheit archivieren, erfahren und zerstören." In *Historische Anthropologie. Kultur Gesellschaft Alltag* 13(1): 121–35.
Chambers, I. 2001. *Culture after Humanism*. London and New York: Routledge.
Chambers, I., and L. Curti, eds. 1996. *The Post-Colonial Question. Common Skies Divided Horizons*. London and New York: Routledge.
Chatterjee, P. 1986. *Nationalist Thought and the Colonial World: A Derivative Discourse*. Minneapolis: University of Minnesota Press.
———. 1993. *The Nation and its Fragments. Colonial and Postcolonial Histories*. Princeton, NJ: Princeton University Press.
———. 2004. *The Politics of the Governed*. New York: Columbia University Press.
Chaturvedi, V., ed. 2000. *Mapping Subaltern Studies and the Postcolonial*. London and New York: Verso.
Chow, R. 1993. *Writing Diaspora. Tactics of Intervention in Contemporary Cultural Studies*. Bloomington and Indianapolis: Indiana University Press.
———. 1994. "Where Have All the Natives Gone?" In *Displacements: Cultural Identities in Question*, edited by A. Bammer, 125–51. Bloomington: Indiana University Press.

———. 2010. "The Politics of Admittance: Female Sexual Agency, Miscegenation and the Formation of Community in Frantz Fanon." In *The Rey Chow Reader*, edited by Paul Bowman, 56–75. New York: Columbia University Press.

Clastres, P. 1974. *La Société contre l'État. Recherches d'anthropologie politique*. Paris: Minuit.

Clavier, P. 2000. *Le Concept du monde*. Paris: Presses Universitaires de France.

Clifford, J. 1988. *The Predicament of Culture. Twentieth-Century Ethnography, Literature, and Art*. Cambridge, MA, and London: Harvard University Press.

———. 1997. *Routes. Travel and Translation in the Late Twentieth Century*. Cambridge, MA, and London: Harvard University Press.

Clifford, J., and G. E. Marcus, eds. 1986. *Writing Culture: Poetics and Politics of Ethnography*. Berkeley: University of California Press.

Coetzee, J. M. 1980. *Waiting for the Barbarians*. London: Secker & Warburg.

———. 1982. *In the Heart of the Country*. London: Penguin Books.

———. 1986. *Foe*. London: Penguin Books.

Cometa, M. 2004. *Dizionario degli studi culturali*, edited by R. Coglitore and F. Mazzara. Rome: Meltemi.

Copjec, J., ed. 1994. *Supposing the Subject*. London and New York: Verso.

Crenshaw, K. 1989. *Demarginalizing the Intersection of Race and Sex: A Black Feminist Critique of Antidiscrimination Doctrine, Feminist Theory and Antiracist Politics*. Chicago: University of Chicago Legal Faculty.

———. 1995. "Intersectionality and Identity Politics: Learning from Violence against Women of Colour." In K. Crenshaw, N. Gotanda, G. Peller, and T. Kendall. *Critical Race Theory*. New York: New Press.

Dal Lago, A., and S. Mezzadra. 2002. "I confini impensati dell'Europa." In *Europa politica. Ragioni di una necessità*, edited by H. Friese, A. Negri and P. Wagner, 143–57. Rome: Manifestolibri.

Davis, M. 2001. *Late Victorian Holocausts. El Niño Famines and the Making of the Third World*. London and New York: Verso.

———. 2006. *Planet of Slums*. London and New York: Verso.

Deleuze, G., and M. Foucault. 1977. "Intellectuals and Power." In *Language, Counter-memory, Practice: Selected Essays and Interviews by Michel Foucault*, edited by D. F. Bouchard, translated by D. F. Bouchard and S. Simon, 205–17. Ithaca, NY: Cornell University Press.

Deleuze, G., F. Guattari. 1983. *Anti-Oedipus. Capitalism and Schizophrenia.* Translated by R. Hurley, M. Seem, and H. R. Lane. Minneapolis: University of Minnesota Press.

———. 1986. *Kafka: Toward a Minor Literature.* Translated by D. Polan, Minneapolis, MN, and London: University of Minnesota Press.

———. 1987. *A Thousand Plateaus: Capitalism and Schizophrenia.* Translated by B. Massumi. Minneapolis, MN, and London: University of Minnesota Press.

Derrida, J. 1967. *De la grammatologie.* Paris: Minuit.

———. 1972. *Marges—de la philosophie.* Paris: Minuit.

———. 1985. "Des Tours de Babel." In *Difference in Translation,* edited by J. F. Graham. Ithaca, NY, and London: Cornell University Press.

———. 1991. *L'autre cap suivi de La démocratie ajournée.* Paris: Minuit.

———. 1994. *Specters of Marx: The State of the Debt, the Work of Mourning and the New International.* Translated by P. Kamuf. London and New York: Routledge.

———. 1996. "Archive Fever: A Freudian Impression." Translated by E. Prenowitz. *Diacritics* 25(2): 9–63.

———. 1998. *Monolingualism of the Other; or, the Prosthesis of Origin.* Translated by P. Mensah: Stanford, CA: Stanford University Press.

———. 2002. *Marx&Sons.* Paris: Presses Universitaires de France-Galilée.

Devi, M. 1981. "Draupadi." *Critical Inquiry* 8(2): 381–402.

Dirlik, A. 2000. *Postmodernity's Histories. The Past as Legacy and Project.* Lanham, MD; Boulder, CO; New York, and Oxford: Rowman & Littlefield Publishers.

Djebar, A. 1992. *Women of Algiers in Their Apartment.* Translated by M. de Jager. Charlottesville: The University Press of Virginia.

Doane, M. A. 1991a. "Film and the Masquerade: Theorizing the Female Spectator." In *Femmes Fatales: Feminism, Film Theory, Psychoanalysis,* 17–32. London and New York: Routledge.

———. 1991b. "Masquerade Reconsidered: Further Thoughts on the Female Spectator." In *Femmes Fatales: Feminism, Film Theory, Psychoanalysis,* 33–43. London and New York: Routledge.

Dussel, E. 1998. "Beyond Eurocentrism: The World-System and the Limits of Modernity." In Jameson and Myoshi, eds. 1998:3–31.

Ehrenreich, B. and Hochschild, A. R., eds. 2003. *Global Woman. Nannies, Maids, and Sex Workers in the New Economy.* New York: Metropolitan Books.

Fabian, J. 1983. *Time and the Other*. New York: Columbia University Press.
Felman, S., and D. Laub. 1992. *Testimony. Crisis of Witnessing in Literature, Psychoanalysis, and History*. London and New York: Routledge.
Fornari, E. 2005. "Subalternità e dissidio. Note filosofiche sul postcoloniale." *Studi culturali* 2(2): 329–40.
Foucault, M. 1972. *The Archaeology of Knowledge*. Translated by A. M. Sheridan Smith. London: Penguin Books.
———. 1977a. *Discipline and Punish: The Birth of the Prison*. Translated by A. Sheridan. New York: Pantheon Books.
———. 1977b. "Nietzsche, Genealogy and History" translated by D. F. Bouchard and S. Simon, in *Language, Counter-memory, Practice: Selected Essays and Interviews by Michel Foucault*, edited by D. F. Bouchard. Ithaca, NY: Cornell University Press.
———. 1979. "The Life of Infamous Men." In *Power, Truth, Strategy*, edited by M. Morris and P. Patton. Sydney: Feral Publications.
Fraisse, G. 1996. *La Différence des sexes*. Paris: Presses Universitaires de France.
———. 2001. *La Controverse des sexes*. Paris: Presses Universitaires de France.
———. 2004. "À côté du genre." In R. Ben Slama, D. Cornell, G. Fraisse, Li Xiao-Jian, S. Niranjana, and L. Waldham. *Masculin\féminin. Pour un dialogue entre les cultures*, 59–84. Paris: Éditions La Découverte.
Fraser, N., and A. Honneth. 2003. *Umverteilung oder Anerkennung?* Frankfurt am Main: Suhrkamp.
Freud, S. 1914. "Erinnern, Wiederholen und Durcharbeiten." In *Internationale Zeitschrift für Ärztliche Psychoanalyse* 2(6): 485–91.
Friedlander, S., ed. 1992. *Probing the Limits of Representation. Nazism and the "Final Solution."* Cambridge, MA, and London: Harvard University Press.
Fuss, D. 1989. *Essentially Speaking. Feminism, Nature and Difference*. London and New York: Routledge.
Gallagher, C., and S. Greenblatt. 2000. *Practicing New Historicism*. Chicago and London: Chicago University Press.
Galli, C. 2001. *Spazi politici. L'età moderna e l'età globale*. Bologna: Il Mulino.
Gilroy, P. 1993. *The Black Atlantic. Modernity and Double Consciousness*. London and New York: Verso.
———. 2003. "Introduzione all'edizione italiana." In *The Black Atlantic. L'identità nera tra modernità e doppia coscienza*. Translated by M. Mellino and L. Barberi. Rome: Meltemi.

———. 2004. *After Empire. Melancholia or Convivial Culture?* London and New York: Routledge.

Ginzburg, C. 1980. *The Cheese and the Worms: The Cosmos of a Sixteenth-Century Miller*. Translated by J. and A. Tedeschi. Baltimore, MD: The Johns Hopkins University Press.

———. 2000. *Rapporti di forza. Storia, retorica, prova*. Milano: Feltrinelli.

Glissant, É. 1989. *Caribbean Discourse: Selected Essays*. Translated by J. M. Dash. Charlottesville: University Press of Virginia.

———. 1996. *Introduction à une poétique du divers*. Paris: Gallimard.

Greenblatt, S. 1991. *Marvelous Possessions. The Wonder of the New World*. Oxford: Clarendon Press.

Guha, R. 1988a. "Preface." In Guha and Spivak, eds. 1988: 35–36.

———. 1988b. "On Some Aspects of the Historiography of Colonial India." In Guha and Spivak, eds. 1988: 37–44.

———. 1988c. "The Prose of Counter-Insurgency." In Guha and Spivak, eds. 1988: 45–88.

———. 1996. "The Small Voice of History." In *Subaltern Studies. Writings on South Asian History and Society*, IX, edited by S. Amin and D. Chakrabarty. New Delhi: Oxford University Press: 1–12.

———. 1997. *Elementary Aspects of Peasant Insurgency in Colonial India*. New Delhi: Oxford University Press.

———. 2002. *History at the Limit of World History*. New York: Columbia University Press.

Guha, R., and G. Ch. Spivak, eds. 1988. *Selected Subaltern Studies*. New York and Oxford: Oxford University Press.

Hall, S. 1990. "Cultural Identity and Diaspora." In *Identity, Community, Culture, Difference*, edited by J. Rutherford. London: Lawrence & Wishart.

———. 1996. "When was 'the Post-colonial'? Thinking at the Limit." In Chambers and Curti, eds. 1996: 242–60.

———. 2006a. *Politiche del quotidiano. Culture, identità e senso comune*, edited by G. Leghissa. Milan: Il Saggiatore.

———. 2006b. *Il soggetto e la differenza. Per un'archeologia degli studi culturali e postcoloniali*, edited by M. Mellino. Rome: Meltemi.

Hannerz, U. 1996. *Transnational Connections. Culture, People, Places*. London and New York: Routledge.

Haraway, D. 1997. *Modest_Witness@Second_Millennium. FemaleMan©_Meets_OncoMouse*. London and New York: Routledge.

Harding, S. 1998. *Is Science Multicultural? Postcolonialism, Feminism, and Epistemologies*. Bloomington and Indianapolis: Indiana University Press.

———, ed. 2004. *The Feminist Standpoint Theory Reader. Intellectual & Political Controversies*. London and New York: Routledge.
Hardt, M., and A. Negri. 2000. *Empire*. Cambridge, MA: Harvard University Press.
Harvey, D. 1990. *The Condition of Postmodernity*. Malden and Oxford: Blackwell.
———. 1996. *Justice, Nature and the Geography of Difference*. Oxford: Blackwell.
———. 2003. *The New Imperialism*. Oxford: Oxford University Press.
———. 2006. *Spaces of Global Capitalism. Towards a Theory of Uneven Geographical Development*. London and New York: Verso.
Heath, S. 1986. "Joan Rivière and the Masquerade." In *Formations in Fantasy*, edited by V. Burgin, J. Donald, and C. Kaplan, 45–61. London and New York: Methuen.
Hegel, G. W. F. 1956. *The Philosophy of History*. Translated by J. Sibree. New York: Dover.
———. 1975. *Aesthetics. Lectures on Fine Arts*. Oxford: Clarendon Press.
Héritier, F. 1996. *Masculin/Féminin. La pensée de la différence*. Paris: Éditions Odile Jacob.
Hobsbawm, E., and T. Ranger. 1983. *The Invention of Tradition*. Cambridge: Cambridge University Press.
Hoffmann, E. 2005. "The Balm of Recognition: Rectifying Wrongs through the Generations." In Owen, ed. 2003: 274–304.
Honig, B. 2001. *Democracy and the Foreigner*. Princeton, NJ, and Oxford: Princeton University Press.
Honneth, A. 1992. *Kampf und Anerkennung. Grammatik sozialer Konflikte*. Frankfurt am Main: Suhrkamp.
Husserl, E. 1954. *Die Krisis der europäischen Wissenschaften und die transzendntale Phänomenologie*. Den Haag: M. Nijhoff.
Jakobson, R. 1971. "On Linguistic Aspects of Translation" in *Selected Writings, II: Word and Language*. The Hague: Mouton & Co.
Jameson, F. 1998. "Notes on Globalization as a Philosophical Issue." In Jameson and Miyoshi, eds. 1998: 54–77.
Jameson F., and M. Miyoshi, eds. 1998. *The Cultures of Globalization*. Durham, NC, and London: Duke University Press.
Koselleck, R. 2004. *Futures Past: On the Semantics of Historical Time*. Translated by K. Tribe. New York: Columbia University Press.
———. 2006. *Begriffgeschichten*. Frankfurt am Main: Suhrkamp.

LaCapra, D. 2001. *Writing History, Writing Trauma*. Baltimore, MD, and London: The Johns Hopkins University Press.
Laclau, E. 1995. *Emancipation(s)*. London and New York: Verso.
Laclau, E. and Mouffe, Ch. 1985. *Hegemony and Socialist Strategy. Towards a Radical Democratic Politics*. London and New York: Verso.
Landry, D., and G. MacLean, eds. 1996. *The Spivak Reader. Selected Works of Gayatri Chakravorty Spivak*. London and New York: Routledge.
Laplanche, J., J.-B. Pontalis. 1988. *The Language of Psychoanalysis*. Translated by D. Nicholson-Smith. London: Karnac.
Laplantine, F. 1999. *Je, nous et les autres, être humain au-delà des appartenances*. Paris: Le Pommier.
Lazarus, N. 1999. *Nationalism and Cultural Practice in the Postcolonial World*. Cambridge: Cambridge University Press.
Lévi-Strauss, C. 1961. *A World On the Wane*. Translated by J. Russell. New York: Criterion Books.
———. 1969. *The Elementary Structures of Kinship*. Translated by J. Harle Bell, J. R. von Sturmer, and R. Needham. London: Eyre & Spottiswoode.
Linebaugh, P., and M. B. Rediker. 2000. *The Many-Headed Hydra: Sailors, Slaves, Commoners and the Hidden History of the Revolutionary Atlantic*. London and New York: Verso.
Loomba, A. 1998. *Colonialism/Postcolonialis*. London and New York: Routledge.
Loraux, N. 1993. "Éloge de l'anachronisme en histoire." *Le genre humain* 27(1): 23–39.
Löwy, M. 2005. *Fire Alarm: Reading Walter Benjamin's "On the Concept of History."* Translated by C. Turner. London and New York: Verso.
Lyotard, J.-F. 1988. *The Differend: Phrases in Dispute*. Translated by G. Van Den Abbeele. Manchester, UK: Manchester University Press.
———. 1991. *The Inhuman: Reflections on Time*. Translated by G. Bennington and R. Bowlby. Cambridge, UK: Polity Press.
Mani, L. 1992. "Cultural Theory, Colonial Texts: Reading Eyewitness Accounts of Widow Burning." In *Cultural Studies*, edited by L. Grossberg, C. Nelson, and P. A. Treichler. London and New York: Routledge.
Marazzi, C. 2008. *Capital and Language: From the New Economy to the War Economy*. Translated by G. Conti. Cambridge, MA: Semiotext(e).

Marramao, G. 2005. *Potere e secolarizzazione. Le categorie del tempo.* Torino: Bollati Boringhieri.
———. 2008. *La passione del presente. Breve lessico della modernità-mondo.* Torino: Bollati Boringhieri.
———. 2012. *The Passage West. Philosophy After the Age of the Nation State.* Translated by M. Mandarini. London and New York: Verso.
Marx, K. 1973. *Grundrisse: Foundations of the Critique of Political Economy.* Translated by M. Nicolaus. Harmondsworth, UK: Penguin Books.
Mbembe, A. 2001. *On the Postcolony.* Berkeley and Los Angeles, CA, and London: University of California Press.
———. 2006. "Qu'est-ce que la pensée postcoloniale? Entretiens avec Achille Mbembe." *Esprit* 12:117–33.
Melandri, E. 2004. *La linea e il circolo. Studio logico-filosofico sull'analogia.* Macerata: Quodlibet.
Mellino, M. 2005. *La critica postcoloniale. Decolonizzazione, capitalismo e cosmopolitismo nei postcolonial studies.* Rome: Meltemi.
———, ed. 2009. *Post-orientalismo. Said e gli studi postcoloniali.* Rome: Meltemi.
Memmi, A. 2004. *Portrait du décolonisé arabo-musulman et de quelques autres.* Paris: Gallimard.
Menchú, R. 1984. *I, Rigoberta Menchú: An Indian Woman in Guatemala.* Translated by A. Wright. London and New York: Verso.
Mezzadra, S., ed. 2004. *I confini della libertà. Per un'analisi politica delle migrazioni contemporanee.* Rome: DeriveApprodi.
———. 2008. *La condizione postcoloniale. Storia e politica nel presente globale.* Verona: ombre corte.
Mezzadra, S., and F. Rahola. 2015. "The Postcolonial Condition: a Few Notes on the Quality of Historical Time in the Global Present." In *Reworking Postcolonialism: Globalization, Labour and Rights*, edited by P. K. Malreddy, B. Heidemann, O. B. Laursen, and J. Wilson, 36–54. Basingstoke, UK, and New York: Palgrave Macmillan.
Mignolo, W. D. 1998. "Globalization, Civilization Processes, and the Relocation of Languages and Cultures." In Jameson and Miyoshi, eds. 1998: 32–53.
———. 2000. *Local Histories/Global Designs. Coloniality, Subaltern Knowledge, and Border Thinking.* Princeton, NJ: Princeton University Press.
Mohanty, Ch. T. 2003. *Feminism Without Borders. Decolonizing Theory, Practicing Solidarity.* London: Duke University Press.
Morrison, T. 1992. *Playing in the Dark: Whiteness and the Literary Imagination.* Cambridge, MA: Harvard University Press.

Mudimbe, V. Y. 1988. *The Invention of Africa. Gnosis, Philosophy, and the Order of Knowledge*. Bloomington and Indianapolis: Indiana University Press.

Nancy, J.-L. 1997. *The Sense of the World*. Translated by J. S. Librett. Minneapolis and London: University of Minnesota Press.

———. 2007. *The Creation of the World or Globalization*. Translated by F. Raffoul and D. Pettigrew. Albany, NY: SUNY Press.

Ngũgĩ wa Thiong'o. 1993. *Moving the Centre. The Struggle for Cultural Freedom*. Oxford: James Currey.

Niranjana, S. 2001. *Gender and Space: Femininity, Sexualization and the Female Body*. New Delhi: Sage.

———. 2004. "Le Genre en générale et en particulier." In R. Ben Slama, D. Cornell, G. Fraisse, Li Xiao-Jian, S. Niranjana, and L. Waldham. *Masculin-féminin. Pour un dialogue entre les cultures*. Paris: Éditions La Découverte.

O'Hanlon, R. 2000. "Recovering the Subject: *Subaltern Studies* and Histories of Resistence in Colonial South Asia." In Chaturvedi, ed. 2000: 72–115.

Ong, A. 2006. *Neoliberalism as Exception. Mutations in Citizenship and Sovereignity*. Durham, NC, and London: Duke University Press.

Ortiz, F. 1995. *Cuban Counterpoint: Tobacco and Sugar*. Translated by H. de Onís. Durham, NC, and London: Duke University Press.

Owen, N., ed. 2003. *Human Rights, Human Wrongs. Oxford Amnesty Lectures 2001*. Oxford: Oxford University Press

Pandey, G. 2000. "Voices from the Edge: The Struggle to Write Subaltern Histories." In Chaturvedi, ed. 2000: 281–99.

Parry, B. 2004. *Postcolonial Studies. A Materialist Critique*. London and New York: Routledge.

Prakash, G. 1990. "Writing Post-Orientalist Histories of the Third World: Perspectives from Indian Historiography." *Comparative Studies in Society and History* 32(2): 383–408.

Pratt, M. L. 1992. *Imperial Eyes. Travel Writing and Transculturation*. London and New York: Routledge.

Rajchman, J., ed. 1995. *The Identity in Question*. London and New York: Routledge.

Rancière, J. 1994. *The Names of History: On the Poetics of Knowledge*. Translated by H. Melehy. Foreword by H. White. Minneapolis and London: University of Minnesota Press.

———. 1999. *Disagreement: Politics and Philosophy*. Translated by J. Rose. Minneapolis and London: University of Minnesota Press.

Remotti, F. 2001. *Contro l'identità*. Rome-Bari: Laterza.
Rhys, J. 1966. *Wide Sargasso Sea*. London: Deutsch.
Ricoeur, P. 2004. *Memory, History, Forgetting*. Translated by K. Blamey and D. Pellauer. Chicago and London: Chicago University Press.
Rigo, E. 2007. *Europa di confine. Trasformazioni della cittadinanza nell'Unione allargata*. Rome: Meltemi.
Rivière, J. 1929. "Womanliness as a Masquerade." *The International Journal of Psychoanalysis* 10: 303–13.
Rushdie, S. 1991. *Imaginary Homelands. Essays and Criticism, 1981–91*. London: Granta Books.
Said, E. W. 1978. *Orientalism*. New York: Pantheon Books.
———. 1983. *The World, the Text and the Critic*. London: Vintage.
———. 1988. *Foreword*. In Guha and Spivak, eds. 1988.
———. 1993. *Culture and Imperialism*. London: Vintage.
———. 1999. *Out of Place*. London: Granta Books.
———. 2000. *Reflections on Exile and Other Essays*. Cambridge, MA: Harvard University Press.
———. 2004. *Humanism and Democratic Criticism*. Basingstoke, UK, and New York: Palgrave Macmillan.
Sarkar, S. 2000. "The Decline of the Subaltern in 'Subaltern Studies.'" In Chaturvedi, ed. 2000: 300–23.
Sassen, S. 1996. *Migranten, Siedler, Flüchtlinge. Von der Massenauswanderung zur Festung Europa*. Frankfurt am Main: Fischer Taschenbuch Verlag.
———. 2001a. "Spatialities and Temporality of the Global: Elements for a Theorization." In *Globalization*, edited by A. Appadurai. Durham, NC, and London: Duke University Press.
———. 2001b. *The Global City*. Princeton, NJ: Princeton University Press.
———. 2006. *Territory Authority Rights. From Medieval to Global Assemblages*. Princeton, NJ, and Oxford: Princeton University Press.
Saussure, F. de. 1959. *Course in General Linguistics*. Translated by W. Baskin. New York: McGraw-Hill.
Schmitt, C. 1950. *Der Nomos der Erde im Völkerrecht des Jus Publicum Europaeum*. Berlin: Duncker & Humboldt. 2nd ed. 1974.
Scholem, G. 1972. *Walter Benjamin und sein Engel*. Frankfurt am Main: Suhrkamp.
Scott, J. W. 1992. "Experience." In Butler and Scott, eds. 1992: 22–40.
———. 1999. *Gender and the Politics of History*. New York: Columbia University Press.

Sen, A. 2003. "Democracy and Its Global Roots." *The New Republic* 229 (14): 28–35.

Shiva, V. 1993. *Monocultures of the Mind. Perspectives on Biodiversity and Biotechnology*. London: Zed Books.

———. 2005. *Earth Democracy: Justice, Sustainability and Peace*. Cambridge, MA: South End Press.

Sloterdijk, P. 2001. *Sphären II. Globen*. Frankfurt am Main: Suhrkamp.

———. 2013. *In the World Interior of Capital. For a Philosophical Theory of Globalization*. Translated by W. Hoban. Cambridge and Malden, UK: Polity Press.

Spivak, G. Ch. 1985. "Feminism and Critical Theory." In Landry and MacLean, eds. 1996: 53–74.

———. 1988. "Subaltern Studies: Deconstructing Historiography." In Guha and Spivak, eds. 1988: 3–34.

———. 1993a. "The Politics of Translation." In *Outside in the Teaching Machine*, 179–200. London and New York: Routledge.

———. 1993b. "More on Power/Knowledge." In *Outside in the Teaching Machine*, 25–52. London and New York: Routledge.

———. 1993c. "Foundations and Cultural Studies." In *Questioning Foundations: Truth/Subjectivity/Culture. Continental Philosophy, V*, edited by H. Silverman, 153–75. London and New York: Routledge.

———. 1993d. "In a Word: Interview." In *Outside in the Teaching Machine*, 1–23. London and New York: Routledge.

———. 1996a. "Scattered Speculations on the Question of Value." In Landry and MacLean, eds. 1996: 107–40.

———. 1996b. "Subaltern Talk. Interview with the Editors." In Landry and MacLean, eds. 1996: 287–308.

———. 1999. *A Critique of Postcolonial Reason. Towards a History of the Vanishing Present*. Cambridge, MA, and London: Harvard University Press.

———. 2000a. "The New Subaltern: A Silent Interview." In Chaturvedi, ed. 2000: 324–40.

———. 2000b. "From Haverstock Hill Flat to U.S. Classroom, What's Left of Theory?" In *What's Left of Theory? New Work on the Politics of Literary Theory*, edited by J. Butler, J. Guillory, and K. Thomas, 1–40. London and New York: Routledge.

———. 2003a. *Death of a Discipline*. New York: Columbia University Press.

———. 2003b. "Righting Wrongs." In Owen, ed. 2003: 168–227.

———. 2008. *Other Asias*. Malden and Oxford, UK: Blackwell.
Taylor, Ch. 1992. *The Politics of Recognition*. Princeton, NJ: Princeton University Press.
Todorov, T. 1981. *Mikhaïl Bakhtine. Le principe dialogique suivi de Écrits du Cercle de Bakhtine*. Paris: Seuil.
Traverso, E. 2006. *Il passato: istruzioni per l'uso. Storia, memoria, politica*. Verona: ombre corte.
Trouillot, M.-R. 1995. *Silencing the Past. Power and the Production of History*. Boston: Beacon Press.
Virno, P. 2015. *Déjà Vu and the End of History*. Translated by D. Broder. London and New York: Verso.
Walcott, D. 1986. *Collected Poems, 1948–1984*. New York: Farrar, Strauss & Giroux.
White, H. 1973. *Metahistory*. Baltimore, MD: The Johns Hopkins University Press.
———. 1987. "The Politics of Historical Interpretation: Discipline and De-Sublimation." In *The Content of the Form. Narrative Discourse and Historical Representation*, 58–82. Baltimore, MD, and London: The Johns Hopkins University Press.
———. 1992. "Historical Emplotment and the Problem of Truth." In Friedlander, ed. 1992: 37–53.
Wolf, E. R. 1982. *Europe and the People without History*. Berkeley: University of California Press.
Young, I. M. 1990. *Justice and the Politics of Difference*. Princeton, NJ: Princeton University Press.
Young, R. J. C. 1990. *White Mythologies. Writing History and the West*. London and New York: Routledge.
———. 1995. *Colonial Desire. Hybridity in Theory, Culture and Race*. London and New York: Routledge.
———. 2001. *Postcolonialism. An Historical Introduction*. Oxford and Malden, UK: Blackwell.
———. 2003. *Postcolonialism. A Very Short Introduction*. Oxford, UK, and New York: Oxford University Press.
Žižek, S., ed. 1994. *Mapping Ideology*. London and New York: Verso.
———. 2002. *Revolution at the Gates: Žižek on Lenin. The 1917 Writings*. London and New York: Verso.

Index of Names

Accarino, Bruno, 99
Adamo, Sergia, 67
Agamben, Giorgio, 30
Ahmad, Aijaz, 66
Albertazzi, Silvia, 128n2
Amselle, Jean-Loup, 128n2, 133n3
Anderson, Benedict, 26
Anzaldúa, Gloria, 83
Appadurai, Arjun, 30, 32–33, 84, 128n1
Arendt, Hannah, 53, 116
Ashcroft, Bill, 128n2, 134n7
Augé, Marc, 30, 51

Bakhtin, Mikhail, 88
Balibar, Étienne, 7, 13–14, 25, 29–31, 80–81, 106, 109–12, 116–17
Bancel, Nicolas, 2, 110
Baraka, Amiri, 32
Barthes, Roland, 59
Bassnett, Susan, 67
Bauman, Zygmunt, 71
Becker-Ho, Alice, 133n5
Beckett, Samuel, 90
bell hooks (Gloria Jean Watkins), 83

Benhabib, Seyla, 84, 109, 116, 117
Benjamin, Walter, 22, 52–53, 55, 57, 81
Bensaïd, Daniel, 70
Berman, Antoine, 72
Beverley, John, 61
Bhabha, Homi, 1, 5, 6, 24, 26–28, 30, 84, 88–90, 92, 111, 115, 117
Blanchard, Pascal, 2, 110
Boccia, Maria Luisa, 118
Brah, Avtar, 133n3
Braidotti, Rosi, 67, 122
Brathwaite, Edward Kamau, 92, 133n6
Brontë, Charlotte, 94
Butler, Judith, 70, 80, 107, 112, 115–16, 121, 124–25

Canclini, Néstor García, 85
Carravetta, Peter, 98
Cavarero, Adriana, 122, 133n6
Certeau, Michel de, 4, 15, 40, 104, 112–13, 127n2, 128n4
Chakrabarty, Dipesh, 5, 6, 18–19, 20, 22–23, 43–45, 50, 53, 55, 57–58, 59, 74–79, 82, 106, 107, 111, 117, 128n3, 131n2

Chambers, Iain, 128n2
Chatterjee, Partha, 17, 23–24, 26, 113–14, 128n3, 129n6
Chaturvedi, Vinayak, 104, 128n2
Chow, Rey, 100, 108, 122–23
Clastres, Pierre, 129n5
Clavier, Paul, 12
Clifford, James, 49, 84, 132n1
Coetzee, John Maxwell, 11, 94–97
Cometa, Michele, 128n2
Coombes, Annie E., 133n3
Crenshaw, Kimberlé, 124
Curti, Lidia, 128n2

Dal Lago, Alessandro, 129n7
Davis, Mike, 29, 60
Defoe, Daniel, 94, 134n8
Deleuze, Gilles, 67–70, 71, 90–91, 98, 127n4
Derrida, Jacques, 19, 27, 40–41, 59, 60, 65, 73–74, 129n5, 132n1, 134n7
Devi, Mahasweta, 101–102
Dirlik, Arif, 66
Djebar, Assia, 103
Doane, Mary Ann, 133n4

Ehrenreich, Barbara, 124
Engels, Friedrich, 20

Fabian, Johannes, 15
Fanon, Frantz, 99, 122, 127n3
Felman, Shoshana, 57
Fichte, Johan Gottlieb, 31
Foucault, Michel, 40, 44, 46–48, 54, 69, 76, 98, 96, 122, 124
Fraisse, Geneviéve, 117, 134n1
Fraser, Nancy, 84

Freud, Sigmund, 40, 54–55, 60, 61, 130n1, 131n4
Friedlander, Saul, 58
Fuss, Diane, 134n2

Gallagher, Catherine, 46–48
Galli, Carlo, 128n1
Gilroy, Paul, xvi, 6, 14, 31–33
Ginzburg, Carlo, 42, 48, 58
Glissant, Édouard, 51–52, 83, 91–93
Gramsci, Antonio, xiii, 6, 37, 74, 79, 98, 104
Greenblatt, Stephen, 46–48
Griffiths, Gareth, 128n2, 134n7
Guattari, Félix, 67–69, 71, 90, 127n4
Guha, Ranajit, 1, 5, 6, 14–17, 36–39, 43, 97, 100, 104, 105, 128n3, 129n5

Hall, Stuart, xvi, 14, 86–87, 115
Hannerz, Ulf, 85
Haraway, Donna, 123
Harding, Sandra, 123
Hardt, Michael, 67
Harvey, David, 69–70
Heath, Stephen, 133n4
Hegel, Georg Wilhelm Friedrich, xii, 4, 6, 15, 16, 21–22, 105, 129n5
Héritier, Françoise, 118
Hobsbawm, Eric, 87
Hochschild, Arlie Russell, 124
Hoffmann, Eva, 62
Honig, Bonnie, 109
Honneth, Axel, 84
Husserl, Edmund, 19

Jakobson, Roman, 73
Jameson, Fredric, 12, 128n1

Kafka, Franz, 90
Kant, Immanuel, xii, 130n1
Klein, Melanie, 126
Koselleck, Reinhart, 5, 21–22

LaCapra, Dominick, 59–60
Laclau, Ernesto, 70, 79–80, 115
Laplanche, Jean, 130n1
Laplantine, François, 133n3
Laub, Dori, 57
Lazarus, Neil, 66
Lemaire, Sandrine, 2, 110
Levi, Primo, 62
Lévi-Strauss, Claude, 56, 119
Linebaugh, Peter, 31
Loomba, Ania, 128n2
Loraux, Nicole, 50, 131n3
Löwy, Michael, 131n1
Lyotard, Jean-François, 35, 42, 99, 132n4

Malinowski, Bronislaw, 85
Mandela, Nelson, 62
Marazzi, Christian, 72
Marcus, George E., 132n1
Marramao, Giacomo, 12, 21, 128n1, 131n3
Marx, Karl, xii, 4, 6, 11, 19–20, 22, 37, 47, 69–78, 104, 123, 128n3
Mbembe, Achille, 15, 31
M'Bokolo, Elikia, 133n3
Melandri, Enzo, 54
Mellino, Miguel, 128n2
Memmi, Albert, 90

Menchú, Rigoberta, 61–62
Mezzadra, Sandro, 54, 70, 108–109, 129n7
Mignolo, Walter D., 15
Mill, John Stuart, 22
Miyoshi, Masao, 128n1
Mohanty, Chandra Talpade, 119
Morrison, Toni, 134n7
Mouffe, Chantal, 79
Mozart, Wolfgang Amadeus, 55
Mudimbe, Valentin Yves, 15

Naipaul, Vidiadhar Surajprasad, 92
Nancy, Jean-Luc, 11–12
Negri, Antonio, 67
Ngũgĩ wa Thiong'o, xvi, 93
Niranjana, Seemanthini, 120, 122

O'Hanlon, Rosalind, 39, 105
Ong, Ahiwa, 71, 109, 115
Ortiz, Fernando, 85

Pandey, Gyanendra, 38
Parry, Benita, 66
Pontalis, Jean-Bertrand, 130n1
Prakash, Gyan, 38, 40
Pratt, Mary Louise, 85–86

Rahola, Federico, 54
Rajchman, John, 134n2
Rancière, Jacques, 6, 44–45, 50, 111–15, 134n1
Ranger, Terence, 87
Rediker, Marcus B., 31
Remotti, Francesco, 132n2
Renan, Ernest, 27
Rhys, Jean, 94
Ricoeur, Paul, 40, 59–60, 62, 131n4

Rigo, Enrica, 109
Rivière, Joan, 133n4
Rousseau, Jean-Jacques, 20
Rushdie, Salman, 83, 92

Said, Edward Wadie, xviii, 1–3, 13, 26, 35–36, 65–66, 79, 127n3
Santner, Eric, 53
Sarkar, Sumit, 104, 128n3
Sassen, Saskia, 29, 109
Saussure, Ferdinand de, 71
Schmitt, Carl, 12
Scholem, Gershom, 131n2
Scott, Joan W., 39, 120
Sen, Amartya, 114
Shiva, Vandana, 114, 125
Sloterdijk, Peter, 4, 13
Spivak, Gayatri Chakravorty, xiii, xiv, 1, 5, 6, 19–20, 36, 66, 73–74, 94, 96–102, 103–104, 105–108, 110, 111, 114, 115–16, 118, 119, 121, 123, 125–26, 128n3, 130n1

Taylor, Charles, 84
Thompson, Edward Palmer, 47
Tiffin, Helen, 128n2, 134n7
Todorov, Tzvetan, 88
Traverso, Enzo, 37
Trivedi, Harish, 67
Trouillot, Michel-Rolph, 41
Tutu, Desmond, 62

Vecchi, Roberto, 128n2
Virno, Paolo, 77

Walcott, Derek, 91–92
White, Hayden, 43–44, 57–61
Wolf, Eric Robert, 15
Woolf, Virginia, 35

Young, Iris Marion, 84
Young, Robert J. C., 13, 36, 54, 66, 67, 69, 73, 84, 104, 128n2

Zimmerman, Marc, 61
Žižek, Slavoj, 54, 70, 75, 80, 99

www.ingramcontent.com/pod-product-compliance
Lightning Source LLC
Chambersburg PA
CBHW021143230426
43667CB00005B/238